LEAVE ME A

Libertarian Education is a small independent publishing collective, which for the past quarter of a century has been campaigning for the development of non-authoritarian initiatives in education.

Also in this series:

Free School, The White Lion Experience, by Nigel Wright, ISBN 0-9513997-1-3.

Freedom in Education: A do-it-yourself guide to the liberation of learning, ISBN 0-9513997-2-1.

No Master High or Low: Libertarian Education and Schooling, 1890-1990, by John Shotton, ISBN 0-9513997-3-X

Real Education: Varieties of Freedom, by David Gribble, ISBN 0-9513997-5-6

The Dredd Phenomenen: Comics and Contemporary Society, by John Newsinger, ISBN 0-9513997-7-2

For the latest information about Libertarian Education, see http://www.libed.org.uk.

LEAVE ME ALONE

POWER, CONTROL AND RESISTANCE IN A PRIMARY SCHOOL

Joanna Stephanie Gore

Libertarian Education

Published by:
Libertarian Education
84b Whitechapel High Street, London E1 7QX.

ISBN 0-9513997-8-0

Copyright: Joanna Gore and Libertarian Education, 2004

Joanna Gore asserts the moral right to be identified as the author of this work.

Front cover by Clifford Harper.

Printed and bound by:
Shortrun Press, Bittern Road, Sowton Industrial Estate, Exeter, EX2 7LW.
(Tel: 01392 211909)

Dedicated to my mum and dad for bringing me up to question.

CONTENTS

Introduction 1
1. What is a Child? 5
2. The School and Myself 9
3. Forms of Control and Resistance to it 19
4. Power and Resistance 39
5. Food for Thought 59
Afterword: The Wider Social Structure/Mental
   Health System 65
Appendix One: Ethical Issues 75
Appendix Two: Summary of Rules and Sanctions 77
References 83

Acknowledgments

I would like to thank all of the staff in the school of my study for putting up with my occasional 'strange' behaviour, the effect that my presence sometimes caused in their class and for answering my probing questions; all of the children for their trust in me, for their persistence in pushing me to try to resist and for letting me take part in their daily friendships, activities and secrets; the parents for parental permission.

I would like to acknowledge the input of my tutors, especially Christina Toren and my supervisor, David Gellner, at Brunel University.

I would like to thank Susan Diab for her editorial input, late night in-depth conversation and her unwavering support; Robert Mitchell for committing himself to provide childcare for the duration of my M.Sc., for the bright look in his eyes during my endless recitations and for my dinner each Thursday night when I got home; David Gribble for his support and editing; George Shaw for his help with final editing; Richard Musgrove and Bar Bowen for their invaluable input.

I would also like to thank Emily Ella Rose Webb-Gore, my daughter, for the constant inspiration from the day she was born, modelling lively, zestful creativity and her uncompromising encouragement and belief in me as a person to make the world a better place for young people.

Joanna Gore

Introduction

My interests as an anthropologist, an artist, a mother and a former child are in how social change comes about and, in particular, what part children play in it. The purpose of this book is to investigate personhood in relation to how children come to resist rather than simply to conform. My hypothesis is that children are not powerless reactors to domination. Rather, they are active agents who participate in social change through an inter-subjective negotiation of ideas of personhood with adults.

For the academic, I lay out the theoretical background of power, resistance, control and socialisation and point to the theoretical stance that I take. For the anthropologist, I detail the fieldwork undertaken in a primary school and analyse the methodological issues that arose, such as the role of participant observer and reflexive power relations. In Appendix One I discuss the ethical issues of consent and confidentiality that I had to consider when researching children. Throughout this book I will use the term "constitution" by this I mean "coming to be" over time, through assimilation of biological, psychological, sociological and emotional experiences. These experiences become a part of the "self" that is "embodied", deeply embedded and instilled with us.

Whilst the child is developing an idea of what an ideal person is, he or she comes to understand, through continual interaction with adults, that most of them have embodied restricted movement and expression. By examining the restriction of movement and expression within a school, where it is deliberately used to encourage children to understand it as an aspect of adulthood, I investigate how this control becomes embodied, and how it is resisted.

I spent much time investigating power and resistance; they are linked both by their opposition and by their similarity in that resistance can be seen as power. Power relations are points of negotiation between adults and children and this means negotiation about ideas of both childhood and adulthood. Through these inter-subjective encounters, power relations and ideas of personhood are in constant flux, negotiation and change.

The child is presented with the idea that the essence of childhood is learning to become like an adult at the same time as being presented with the idea of what a child is. However, the child does not simply passively conform but resists what society says that they are. I demonstrate how the child does this through everyday forms of resistance, and consider then how this plays a part in the social construction of the self and others.

The book is intended to be accessible to the non-specialist. Most of the academic comment is in the form of footnotes and I hope the children's own words will go a long way towards exposing the education system in all its absurdity.

There are two appendices. The first is about the ethical issues of research with children; the second gives the summary of the behavioural rules and sanctions at the school that I studied. In addition, there is an afterword that discusses the similarities between the education system and the mental health system, and shows how children and people labelled as having mental health problems are marginalised, oppressed and resist in much the same way.

The purpose of the book is to investigate: children's different forms of resistance; how they use power themselves; how they are controlled by institutional power; how power and resistance are constituted over time; and how, in spite of their apparent powerlessness, children play a part in social change, whilst remembering the wider socio-political environment that these structures and institutions are embedded within.

A Technical Note on Power and Resistance

Resistance as a notion is problematic in that it can also be regarded as a form of power; as Abu-Lughod (1990) argues, we can learn much about strategies and structures of power by analysing resistance. I suggest that we can also learn much about resistance by analysing power, as I have done in this book.

Resistance can easily be romanticised; the subordinate is romanticised as the totally innocent powerless victim of oppression in need of liberation. This naively positions the subordinate as totally and always powerless, which is clearly not the case when we study resistance. However, when power is considered as everywhere, and therefore used by everybody, the oppression of subordinate groups and their acts of resistance can be lost. If the act of resistance is a harnessing of power, the subordinate can no longer be considered oppressed. This then denies the existence of oppressive systems that do clearly exist. To avoid getting trapped in the romance of resistance while also avoiding the negation of oppressive systems, power and resistance must be studied together as complex networks, not as a simple binary construct.

I have demonstrated how, in a primary school, power and resistance are constantly in flux in relation to those who are at that time exercising it.

This supports Foucault's theory of power being everywhere and the theory of everyday resistance to power expounded by Scott.

1. What is a Child?

The key to the oppression that faces young people is the division between adults and children. It was decided some time ago that children were different from adults. Somehow they were not civilised, cultured, socialised. They needed teaching to become complete people (as defined by their own culture). This concept of children as separate and different from adults seems to be a universal one.

The division is based on the idea that children are not yet people. Society, through everyday socialisation and conditioning, turns children into people (adults) of their particular culture. Being an adult encompasses being granted the rights of a member of one's society. Each society marks an age at which this happens. In the West it is between sixteen and twenty-one years old, in some other places ten or eleven. Before this time one is not considered to be a "person", and the younger one is the less of a "person" one is. This is the justification for not giving children equal rights, for example the right to vote, to work and to have economic autonomy and freedom. It is the justification for children's oppression.

The oppression of children is vicious. No other group of human beings is stripped of its rights in such a ruthless but deemed-acceptable manner. Children are treated as non-persons. Imagine an adult in a supermarket having to ask a companion for twenty pence to buy something and getting hit for asking, or having to ask permission to go to the toilet. Imagine it being illegal for you to walk around outside between 9:00 am and 3:30 pm, and any other person being able to call the police and have you picked up if you did. Imagine somebody "grounding" (imprisoning) you for swearing. Imagine having no protection in law when somebody physically attacks you. Imagine seeing notices put up on doors that say you are not allowed in: "Children and dogs not allowed." Signs excluding Jews and dogs were put up on doors in Nazi Germany. During apartheid it was acceptable to put up signs forbidding blacks to enter. And in this country until very recently it was acceptable to prevent women from entering various establishments. Thankfully, people have seen the error in these ways, and such persecution for being a member of a particular group, whether defined by class, colour, religion or sex, is seen as absurd and gross misconduct on the part of those advocating it. Unfortunately persecution for being the wrong age has been overlooked.

Imagine being forced by law to go every day to an institution where people make you stand in lines, sit on the floor and listen for hours to talk that is of no interest to you; where they restrict your movement, shout at you, and punish you for speaking or being lively; where they take away your 'privileges' (your freedom, your clothes or your belongings) for saying what you think. The fact that basic human rights are called privileges, when applied to children, is telling in itself. In order to oppress children and to allow these atrocities to go on with a clear conscience, we adults must dehumanise children - we say they are not yet people, hence the category "child".

The segregation of children and adults is the most widespread segregation I know of in the world. In the past there were tribes and societies that treated children almost as equals or certainly with much less hierarchy, 'protection' and categorical division than we have become used to in modern societies. For example the Trobrianders studied by Malinowski (1932) were confused at the notion of authority over young members of the tribe and appalled at the idea of punishing them when suggested by him. Special huts were constructed in the village to allow children to partake in sex play with each other at ages as young as five as this was considered a healthy part of their everyday life experience. These societies have died out as the West has imposed its hegemony on the rest of the world. Children are seen as beings that are becoming persons, not ones that already are whole and complete. Childhood is a concept created to confuse and divide us.[1] The lie is that we will "grow up". We yearn to be older, to be considered whole, to feel better than those younger than us. Toddlers are already aspiring to be children; teens hate to be treated like children (lower class). Childhood is not biologically given. Viewing 'childhood' as a condition of being, rather than a constructed category that people inhabit, leads to a view of children as beings that are "becoming" rather than ones that already are (James, Jenks and Prout, 1998).

Protection is Oppression

A key aspect of the oppression of children is protection. Because children are considered to be not whole but "becoming", and therefore fragile and innocent, we accept the idea that they need protecting and use it as a

---

1   I agree with James, Jenks and Prout (1998) in arguing that the category "childhood" is a socially constructed category, in that it is not biologically given.

socially acceptable form of oppression. Under the guise of 'taking care' of them, 'looking after' them, 'protecting' them, children are prevented from making decisions for themselves and doing things deemed perfectly acceptable for adults. The adult's ownership and control of a child's body and mind in practice and law is assumed in the name of this protection. Protection is a disguised form of oppression. It is the sugar that helps the medicine go down. It is a way of preventing children from having access to the adult world.

Before the women's movement, this protective oppression was often extended to women, preventing many of them from working, doing certain physical activities, using their intelligence or voting, for example. We have learnt that women are powerful, intelligent and useful participants in society once their oppression has been lifted. The same is true of children.[2]

If we spent less time trying to "produce" human beings and trusted young people as producers, letting them grow naturally with love and

---

[2] Bourdieu (1997) explains the process of socialisation as the emergence of the habitus, a complex network of structures and categorisations that constitute our environment; however, this theory does not account for societal change. Piaget, on the other hand, argues that these structures are self-regulating and transforming (Piaget, 1971) - as each new piece of information meets this network of structures it triggers a shift in all the others. The constitutional process is both continuous and transformational. As Merleau-Ponty explains in his study of time and space, these structures become instilled and embedded deeply within us through everyday lived experience (Merleau-Ponty, 1962). I argue, in line with Toren (1993), that "coming to be" is a micro-historical process and as such encompasses all aspects of what we are: social, psychological and biological beings. Throughout this overall historical constitution of ourselves we are functioning in inter-subjective relations with others. Although we embody all that it is to be a person of our specific culture, we are also still self-organising and self-creating because structures are also self-creating and transforming; this accounts for societal change. In the same way children are both products and active producers of society, as they also partake in inter-subjective relations with others. Structure and agency go hand in hand informing each other. This means that it is important to remember that, even though children are active agents in social production, they also hold much less power than the adult agents and the institutional structures within which they spend much of their time making meaning.

support, I believe we would find that we had generations of new, fresh, flexible, inventive and creative thinkers who would enhance our societies.

2. The School and Myself

I decided to study two well-separated age groups within a single primary school to enable me to compare how resistance and power relations develop and change over time in an institutional setting. One class was of the oldest children ranging from ten to eleven years old (the juniors) and the other was a reception class of the youngest children ranging from four to five years old (the infants). Dockbridge is generally seen in the community as an "alternative" school with a friendly and relaxed ethos. There is no school uniform because the school believes that one's dress is an important way of expressing one's individuality. There is a wide representation of ethnic origins in both staff and children, and sixteen different languages are spoken in the school.

Dockbridge is not considered strict, the emphasis being on the development of the child's personal growth and social relationships rather than academic achievement. The teachers that work there accept this ethos, and there are more male teachers than is usual for primary schools. The classes at Dockbridge are relatively small, varying from sixteen to twenty-five.

The Classes and Daily Structure

There are six year-groups in the school after the nursery and two reception classes. After transition from nursery through to reception, the children move into year one, two and eventually to year six. At the beginning of the year, the class teacher and the headteacher balance the classes in terms of number and gender. The classes in each year are identified by their class teacher's name, for example Trudy's class, Luke's class. Most of the teachers are called by their first names, but some are called by their surnames, for example Mr Grain, Miss Drake. This seems to vary according to the teacher's personal preference.

In the morning, children are supposed to arrive at 8.55 a.m. (although many do not) and go to their classes where the register is taken at 9.10 a.m. At this time they are to get books down from the shelf, sit on the carpet and read. The infants are read to in small groups, with some children doing individual reading. This process also applies each time they come in from break. The juniors will then do some work, usually English.

Before assembly, the infants do a bit of "carpet-time learning" - Janet (an infant teacher) referred to this as learning time - and then some table-based work. Assembly is usually from 10.30 to 10.45, and then there is a break until 11 am. Work time for the juniors goes on until dinner time at 12.30. The infants have dinner at 12.00 so that they are out of the hall in time for the "big ones" to come in. Lunch goes on until 1.30. The Rangers (see later) have their lunch early with the infants when they are on duty. From 2.30 until 3.00 the infants have another break that the juniors do not have, and at 3.30 all of the children go home. This is the formal structure of the day. However many things go wrong and extra activities are sometimes added which change the timetable. For example, if the line in the playground is not straight enough, pupils may have to wait up to 20 minutes before going in to lunch; rainy days may prevent playtime; and there may be trips out of school.

Hierarchy from Headteacher to the Nursery

The school has a formal hierarchy, with the headteacher at the top. She manages the school's finance, the staff and the overall logistics of the school, deals with the local authorities and governors and intervenes in disciplinary problems that teachers and administrative staff are not able to deal with. She is seen as the "big boss" by the children; they do not want to be sent to her, even though, on the occasions that they meet her informally on trips or school celebration days, they are fairly relaxed with her as she is an approachable, friendly person. It is really the idea of her position that is feared and used as a threat to the children. The deputy head is portrayed in a similar way, although she is also the special needs teacher and generally spends more time in direct contact with the children, for example in assemblies and covering for absent teachers.

The next layer down in the hierarchy is made up of the teachers, who spend most of their time in class, but sometimes go out on playground duty; usually they spend their breaks in the staff room. The children resent this as they complain that they are out in the cold and are not allowed sugar in their drinks, while the teachers have sugary tea and biscuits and are warm and cosy indoors. Then there are the secretaries/receptionists who exercise some discipline and also ask the children to do jobs for them. They control access in and out of the school, registers, dinner money and general administration, and are the point of contact between the outside and the inside world.

Finally come the staff helpers, who are employed for classroom support and dinner hall duty. Dinner duty entails supervising the children as they line up, keeping the line quiet and making sure the children fill up the tables in the right order. The helpers also control noise level and movement by using rewards and punishments; they can decide who gets seconds, and they can keep children in; they may shout at them and there is a less confrontational custom of giving a vase of flowers for the infants' quietest table. Helpers also do playground duty, which entails surveying the playground for misbehaviour, such as climbing through the playhouse windows, climbing the tree, swearing or fighting, and attending to children who get hurt or need to go to the toilet.

Long-time employees of the school also have a certain amount of power in making decisions. Such staff are the premises manager, the computer technician and the administrator who organises trips, events and the storeroom. Next come the dinner ladies who make and serve food. They do not discipline the children but hold power in that they can give you more food and more seconds if they like you or happen to know your mum. Then come the Rangers - specially selected older children who have a uniform (a Ranger hat) to identify them. The job entails taking responsibility for bringing out board games and organising group games in the playground. They are also expected to sort out disputes if they feel they can. They hold power over the other children as they say who plays which games and the helpers will usually, but not always, back them up if they can't sort a dispute out. Next are the older children in the school who hold power by their size and age; however a more complex hierarchy also exists which is governed by popularity, which will be discussed later. The youngest children in the school have least authority. However they mock and tease the children in the nursery and sometimes each other for being "babies".

Peter shouts out, 'My mum said Edward is a baby, but he's not, is he Janet?' Edward starts to cry. Janet says 'No you're fine, aren't you Edward? Oh dear, don't get upset.' Peter is confused as he can see that Edward is not a baby but his mum has said he is, whereas Janet and George both understand it as a derogatory term.

Field notes, 1999, Infants class

Professional qualifications legitimise authority and worth. The worth of helpers is not so clear and has to be demonstrated by how well they control the children and how smoothly that they can make things run. The Rangers' authority is signified by the Ranger hat and legitimised by the job title given to them by those further up the hierarchy.

Interviews

I conducted and taped group interviews with twenty juniors. In order to try to reduce the power relations between myself (as an adult) and them (as children), I interviewed groups of four to five children, which gave them the support of their peers. I was aware that the questions anthropologists ask in interviews can influence the data collected, so I conducted the interviews in the form of guided discussions within the group, getting the children to talk around the relevant area. I gave them a list of open questions, which they read before deciding on the ones they wanted to discuss. This meant they took the lead, taking the conversation in the direction most significant to them, while at the same time I kept it around the themes by steering it back if it went completely off track. I conducted the interviews in the "library", where the children felt comfortable and were not afraid of teachers overhearing them, as the library was not staffed and was also used for a variety of other activities such as art projects.

I didn't formally interview the infants but I talked to them informally throughout the day; otherwise I thought it might be too similar to carpet/learning time where they were used to having to guess the 'right' answer.

Participant Observation

Ball (1983) argues for the importance of recognising institutional time and how the timing of research is often determined by the researcher's personal timetable. He says that this affects the data collected and is not always taken into account. My research was determined in these ways as the timing fitted into my personal study for a Master's degree. However, studying the juniors at the very end of their primary education was significant when analysing resistance, as I suggest that this is the point in primary school that resistance is most outstanding; the children are at their eldest, have had experience of restrictions and resistance. They have also taken some responsibility over the younger ones, and have therefore gained an insight into holding power over others in the institutional setting. I am not suggesting that studying the rest of the school year would not have been useful for comparison. However, due to the restriction of available time, I believe this was the best time to study resistance.

In order to get as much variety as possible, in addition to the many days in school doing what the children did, I went on two school trips to the seaside, one to the local maritime museum, to the local library, to the playground opening day, to a school disco, to a culture share evening, a parents' meeting, the school leavers' assembly, the headteacher's leaving assembly and the headteacher's leaving party. I also hung around outside the school gates with the juniors quite a bit before and after school.

I spent three months in the school taking notes as a participant observer. A participant observer intends to participate in the society/culture in which she studies whilst observing that society. This is done with the intention of becoming as much as possible "as one" with the people so that the researcher's presence becomes ignored or accepted and therefore unobtrusive. It is always debated as to how much of a participant one can become in a different culture as the researcher's presence always effects the environment. Therefore this is reduced in as many ways as possible, for example by doing, speaking, acting and inhabiting the same spatial, auditory, hierarchical constructs. The length of research also affects this.

I recorded the structure and functions of daily activities with the intention of following and experiencing a day in the life of a primary school pupil. In order to come to understand the negotiation of power relations between adults and children, I looked at the interactions between adults and children and among the children themselves. I also looked at how children resist domination by breaking rules and creating or taking part in forbidden activities such as swearing games, and how they recognised and pushed the boundaries of restrictions, for example in daring games and direct negotiation with adults. I mapped the space in which the child's day was lived, to what extent the child commanded the space in relation to others, for example in line, moving down corridors, in the classroom and playground. I also paid particular attention to restriction of movement and differential access. I focused on symbols as condensed expressions of meaning, for example the blue band which one had to wear to show one had permission to be out of class and moving around the rest of the school.

At first my notebook caused the children to think of me as a teacher taking down naughty children's names, because a teacher was often posted in assembly with an A4 book to do this and therefore identify and punish offenders. However, I had a small book and the children soon learned that there were no repercussions when I wrote about them.

Least Adult Role

As an anthropologist, I advocate the participant observer role, although I recognise that people from a different culture or life experience can never completely be as (that is act like/embody/become) those they study. The only way one could be a complete participant in this manner would be to study somebody of one's own culture, sex, age and class. Participant observers minimise the differences between themselves and those they study by, for instance, learning the language, wearing the same clothes, acting and moving similarly, taking on similar physical manifestations and abiding by the same codes and practices.

Even though the adult researcher in a school may try to cast aside all aspects of adult superiority the child being studied may not. The child will always know that the researcher as an adult is there by choice, whereas the children are not; the child cannot leave, the researcher can. The adult is not picked up by a parent at the end of the day and the receptionist will let out any adult who requests it; this is, of course, not how the child experiences the world. The child knows that the adult is playing at being a child, rather than really being one. To presume that the child will simply lose sight of this, because the researcher sits on the floor with her and plays with the sand, is to presume that the child has not embodied or retained the normal concept of the self and other; it is to presume that children do not to situate themselves in the category of child, and, in this case, the 'other' in the category of adult. In fact the child has already embodied, through the process of making meaning of everyday lived experiences, what it is to be a child or an adult and this cannot then simply be cast aside.

However, I do believe, as an anthropologist, that it is vital to break down as many differences as one can. It is helpful to minimise the difference in power between the adult researcher and the child. I think this is best achieved by not exerting authority roles explicitly or implicitly, and as far as possible by sharing the child's space. It is not that you are pretending to be a child but that you are letting the children know that you are trying to understand as much as you can of what it is to experience childhood.

Marginalisation is unavoidable; equating oneself with the children limits access to the data from adults in the same way that equating oneself with adults limits access to data from children. I decided to be a semi-participant observer through friendship. I ate in the dinner hall with the children. I didn't go into the staff room. I sat on the floor in assemblies. I didn't tell children off when they did something 'wrong'. And I learned their dance techniques at the disco. The fact that I showed no adult disapproval normally meant that the children were remarkably free with language and actions that were usually restricted around the teachers and helpers; they would swear in front of me and "diss" (insult) teachers. I made it clear that I did not have an authoritative role and that I was "on their side." I agreed with their repeated complaints and insults about a particularly loud and aggressive helper. The children enjoyed helping me out like a new girl, and got a sense of significance in telling me what to do; their knowledge of school procedures far outweighed mine. They taught me, for instance, in what order to pick up one's tray, cutlery and food, and also where and how to sit in the dinner hall. As a result, I believe I was trusted by the children as a friend and let into many of their secret realms of being.

To those who knew me, I was not generally equated with the adults in the school. What role I did hold was more ambiguous. For instance an infant asked me, "Are you a teacher, a child or a mum?" And one day a junior asked me, "Are you going to be a writer when you grow up - I mean leave university?"

A child runs up to me and says, "Hey miss he sweared.'. Another boy says, "She's not a teacher." He says again, "He sweared." I say, "I don't care." The other boy says, "See I told ya, she's not a teacher."
Field notes, 1999, Infants class

When I was asked by a child to reprimand another, or when a child told me about somebody breaking a rule, for example, "John is climbing on the tree," I would smile and say, "Oh yes." Children tended to presume I had status as an adult/authority figure until I proved otherwise.

Before long, the children expected me to obey the rules that they had to obey, which didn't apply to teachers and helpers.

There is not enough room on the table and Edward is trying to find out who's been on the longest so that he can swap with them. He goes around the table asking, "Have you been on this table a long time?" All of the children say, "No." I have been there the longest so when he asks me I say, "Yes." He then says, "You have to get off then, so that I can have your chair because it's my turn."
Field notes, 1999, Infants class

Here Edward (an infant) was treating me as he would have treated another infant; the rule applied to me in the same way as to all of the other children; he would not have said this to his teacher. Edward was a child who accepted me as of equal standing; he ignored me if I suggested he do something, he called me names such as "bum" or "bum-face", and had an annoying habit of hitting me. Once he came up to me and slapped my face very hard with both hands. When I shouted, "Ow!" and objected, he ran off, laughing and mocking me.

I found that the juniors were generally more accepting of me as an "equal friend" and were less likely to expect me to take on adult roles. Infants, for instance, might ask me to tie their shoelaces. This was because the juniors were older, more physically competent and simply larger - many of the children were at least as tall as I was. I was also able to talk about experiences that we shared; Margaritte, for instance, talked to me about how to get a boyfriend and advised me on what to wear to a nightclub to attract the "sexy boys".

There were also instances where I was treated as an adult, much to the juniors' confusion. For instance, I was given twice as much dinner as they were and they complained about this indignantly, shouting, "Oh, that's not fair." I agreed that this was unfair, but I didn't give my dinner up.

Having my daughter in the school was useful at break times as she kept on "showing off" to the others how she could swear in front of me, her mum, without being reprimanded. This gave the juniors more confidence in pushing and testing me and playing with the power relationship.

The infants were more confused about my role as a non-adult figure.

> *When playing with plastic animals, if I pick up one and play with it in the same indulgent way that they do [making loud animal noises and making it run] they all stop and watch me as it is out of context for an adult to do this in school.*
>
> **Field notes, 1999, Infants class**

This was useful as it exposed the importance of the context of adult behaviours. Had I simply been acting as a conventional adult I would not have gained this insight. I was careful, however, not to be an adult who was simply acting inappropriately. For example, I would take a child to the toilet, and was kind when a child fell over, finding a teacher or a helper to sort it out.

There were times when I also found myself in the adult sphere. For instance, on the seaside trip, due to the seating arrangements, I had to sit amongst the teachers and I found conversation surprisingly easy, as most generally talked about the children. When I was with both children and adults, the adults tended to ignore me, probably because when with the children, I tended to be on the same spatial level as they were, sitting on the floor, while the adults talked to each other over our heads. It may also have been due to the fact that I talked more to the children and often had my head buried in my notebook. Adults are less likely to interrupt this than children.

The adults also sometimes tried to place me in a role I was reluctant to take, by for instance giving me adult responsibility over the children.

> *Today is the first day I have been equated with the adults; I have been given responsibility for looking after some of the infants [walking around the museum with them]. This is also the first time that Clare [adult helper] talked to me. John refuses to come with me. He runs off and when I chase him and try to hold his hand he simply lies down. I stand there a bit useless until Janet comes back and tells him to get up. He does and she holds his hand giving me Zainab instead. Janet is a bit annoyed with me and my lack of authoritative control over the children, as I am not much help to her.*
> **Field notes, 1999, Infants class**

I believe the semi-participant role was useful, as I gained insight into both adults' and children's experience, and was often hovering in-between, a useful place to occupy when studying interactive power relations.[1]

---

1 As Laerke remarks, "Because I was an adult seeking to escape my own adult authority, I became a double misfit, as it were, placed right at the centre of on-going exchanges of domination and subordination between adults and children." (Laerke, 1998, p. 4)

3. Forms of Control and Resistance to it

Forms of control and resistance to it can be both overt and covert. Control becomes embodied through the restriction of movement within space, the displaying of dominance, spatial control, differential access to space and restriction of noise. Resistance forms in reaction to such restrictions.

Considering how many forms of everyday resistance happen on a minute-to-minute basis, there were surprisingly few incidents of direct confrontation between children and teachers. When it did happen, direct resistance incited much excitement, discussion and movement in the school amongst the children and was hushed up as embarrassing and shocking by the teachers. The children talked about stories of expelled pupils with astonished excitement.

"It's horrible when a teacher shouts in your face. I want to hit them. Spit goes in your face and stuff."

"Has anyone ever hit a teacher?"

"Yeh, Lou has, and John kicked Mrs Grey in the stomach. They got suspended."

"Lou hit Ms Marsh with a chair."

"Yeh, and Clare, she poked a pencil right through Kirsten's [a helper] hand."

"They were brave, man."

"That's good." [Shaking his head in disbelief]

Field notes, 1999

Embodied Action

Embodied action is action that has become so ingrained within the self that it is no longer consciously thought about, it is simply done. An English child who uses a knife and fork to eat, on seeing a Moroccan eating with his fingers, asks, "Why does he eat with his fingers?", rather than, "Why do I eat with these implements?" Imagine an adult skipping down the street. People would think that looks pretty weird, they would not generally ask how did it happen that I and everybody else walks down the street in this particularly standard way, with both our arms down and moving just so. Or how did it happen that I think it is normal for a child to skip but not an adult? We have embodied the actions that we have constituted as normal for our society.

Legitimised by the formal structure of the school and practised through the everyday routine of repetitive actions, power relations become embodied within the self. The infants were generally thought of as less capable of sitting still than the juniors were, therefore, in the reception class, there was much emphasis on bodily control. This was implemented by instructions and commands such as "hands on head", "fingers on lips", "back straight", "bottoms on the carpet", "legs crossed" and "eyes on Janet". Many songs and games also reinforced this, for example, "Head, shoulders, knees, and toes" and "Simon says". Children were not allowed to speak unless they had their hands up and were given permission; children who shouted out the right answer were ignored by the teacher in favour of ones who had put their hands up. (Even so some children persisted in shouting out and sometimes did get listened to.) By the time a child joined the juniors, much of this type of physical control had abated as the required behaviour had been sufficiently embodied.

The embodiment of such constructs was shown by the way the children (especially the juniors) moved around the school. They walked in line and it looked as though they were not aware of what they were actually doing with their bodies. Of course they were, but they went through the actions that the teachers expected, while simultaneously carrying on their own conversations and activities with their peers. A child might be facing the back of the line deep in animated conversation with a friend; however she would notice and follow the person who had moved in front of her in line without stopping talking. Juniors would go into the classroom, get a book from the shelf without looking and sit on the carpet, all of the while still engrossed in conversation with their friends. The infants were also to a certain extent able to do this but were more likely to wander off and forget the routine they were supposed to be following. Juniors would be following the routine at the same time as sharing sherbet out, playing with and hiding toys, fighting with the opposite sex or throwing things across the room, for example. Being an adult, and therefore somebody who had embodied much more of the required decorum, I found it difficult to join in. I found that I was far more trained to listen to the teacher, and really had to fight feelings of guilt and fear if I was to sit and chat about boyfriends with the girls while the teacher was addressing us. The children had also learnt to answer questions the teacher asked when addressing the whole class without actually listening. Teachers would often say, for example, "Did everybody understand that?", "Is everybody ready?" or "Can everybody hear me?" The children automatically shouted "Yeees" in unison, even though they obviously hadn't listened to a word. This indicates why children, once they were ready to work, often asked each other and the teacher what they were supposed to do even though the purpose of carpet-time had been to explain exactly this. The automatic "Yeeees" was in response to a question; they could tell by the tone that the required response was "yes" and so did not need to listen to what was actually being said.

> *It is wet play and the children are in the hall. They have been brought in because it is raining. There is much noise and commotion from the children as there are lots of them in the hall together, and the flavour is 'playtime', not assembly. They have been sat down ready to watch television but there is too much noise for them to hear. It seems quite obvious to me that they don't actually want to watch television, otherwise they would be looking at it and trying to listen. Zenobi [helper] shuts the doors to the television. "Do you want to watch this telly?" The children in unison shout "yeees" [long and drawn out]. This happens many times. At one point Graham [helper] comes in and shouts in a deep voice for them to be quiet. He takes one boy out and shouts at him outside about listening to the video. Three children have now been sat facing the wall as a punishment for making too much noise. Graham comes in and sits in the middle of the children on a chair as a menacing force. When break is over Zenobi says, "Did you enjoy that?" The children shout in unison "Yeees." It is quite obvious that only about fifteen children out of about one hundred could actually hear the television, most could not see it or were having conversations or playing games, however they still all shouted "Yeees." This pleased Zenobi as this is the response she wanted and everybody left for class.*
>
> **Field notes, 1999, Infants class**

The infants were not as adept at chatting while appearing to do what the teacher said. It was easy to see when they were having conversations of their own and the teacher stopped them. They had not yet learnt how to do it discreetly.

Children appeared to learn this embodied action over time. Because the infants were not going through the motions correctly they needed to be stopped and redirected all of the time. This was done via the constant restriction of their movement (as above). One particular mechanism used with the infants was to play a version of "Simon says". The children learnt only to follow instructions that started with "Janet says". If they were caught out following an instruction that did not start with "Janet says", they were pointed out and laughed at.

> The children are sitting on the carpet. Janet says, "Janet says hands on head." The children follow. "Janet says stand up." They stand up. "Janet says stand on one leg." She then says, "Sit down." Noel sits down. Janet and all of the children point at Noel and laugh. He smiles, gets up and sits by Janet because he is now out of the game.
>
> **Field notes, 1999**

He had not only been ridiculed for not 'obeying' correctly; he had also been punished in that he was now excluded from the game. The game was played faster and faster, building up the children's skills in listening to and following instructions, whilst also assimilating who is the one they must listen to and obey.

Janet used the same voice later when we came in after lunch. She said, "Hands on heads, bottoms on the carpet, eyes on Janet." The children, still in the mood of the game, rushed to be the first to do it. The assimilation of adult as instructor and child as instructed is so familiar that comical situations such as this one below occasionally occur demonstrating it.

> We are sitting on the carpet ready to do choosing time. Much chatting is happening between the children. Janet sits down and instructs in a loud clear voice, "Noel, put your hand up." Noel immediately puts his hand straight up in the air, his back goes straight and he looks directly attentively at Janet. We all look at him and then at Janet to see why she has said this. Janet says, "I don't know why I said that. It's OK, Noel, you can put your hand down." Everybody looks confused, including Janet. I laugh, then Janet laughs and the children follow.
>
> **Field notes, 1999, Infants class**

Janet was so used to saying, "Put your hand up", it had become automatic, and Noel was so used to following instructions from Janet that he did not question this out of context behaviour, he just obeyed. This is not to say, however, that these power relations are not contested; they are, on both individual and collective levels. The kinds of behaviour that do not conform or that contest power relations would include not responding or simply refusing to communicate. Children often try to make the exercise of power over them as difficult as possible by unresponsive movement, obeying as slowly as possible ("dragging their feet", as Scott identified in peasants' behaviour in *Weapons of the Weak: Everyday Forms of Peasant Resistance*) or refusing to look at the teacher or to hear what is said.[1] They may also refuse to respond physically; as teachers are no longer allowed to use force or to punish children physically this lack of response can be a powerful tool for resistance.

Khalid, when told to get up and work, stays still. When Janet tries to talk to him he puts his head in his arm so that she cannot see his face. She tries to pull his arm away but his body moves with it so she still cannot speak to his face. Janet is being careful as to how much physical force she can use and Khalid is aware of this. She asks, "Do you not want to do any work?" He says, "No." She says he can do something else after he has done a bit and drags him up onto his feet. He sits in a chair at Clare's table. Khalid is very unresponsive. Clare [infant helper] gives him an object to draw round, as asking him does not get a response. She shouts at him to draw around a pingpong ball and says, "Do it carefully." He is looking the other way, obviously defying the instruction. She gives him two more objects to draw round. As he is looking in the opposite direction and not doing it she has to take his hand, put a pencil in it, and direct his hand around the object. His fingers become limp and he drops the pencil. She picks it up and puts it back in his hand, directing it again. Clare eventually gives up as Khalid is physically useless like this and asks him what he would like to do. He says, "Bricks." He jumps up and runs off with some enthusiasm and life back in his body.

Field notes, 1999, Infants class

Spatial Control

Merleau Ponty, in his study of time and space, shows us how over time we embody our environment. The use of space is very important to this developmental process. For example, we have come to understand the structure and function of a lecture theatre. If you are in the audience, you sit and listen to the person standing facing you at the front unless invited to speak. If the lecturer were to sit on the floor facing the opposite

---

1   As Silverman, Baker and Keogh point out, "Silence (or at least lack of verbal response) allows children to avoid implication in the collaboratively accomplished adult moral universe and thus, as is shown in other chapters in this book, enables them to resist the way in which an institutional discourse serves to frame and constrain their social competencies." (1998, p. 220)

direction, or a member of the audience were to stand on the table and address the ceiling, this behaviour would be out of context for that space. And so, to a certain extent, the space we are in governs our behaviour in that space. Power is always displayed, so that others will know where the power lies. In schools power is displayed in the use of differential access to space, the use of particular objects such as chairs, which may imply status, and restrictions on movement and behaviour.

Hierarchical relations are informed by the use of space. Chairs indicate where you are in the hierarchy - small chairs are for the youngest children, and the size of your chair increases with your status until you become an adult with a big, square, comfy chair in your classroom.

Juniors fight for the biggest chairs in their room and often sit on their teacher's chair as a form of defiance.

> *The children come in. Greg and David take two chairs from Hilret's desk, as they are bigger chairs. Hilret then takes one from Emma's desk, Emma takes one from Luke's desk, Luke tries to take one from Richard's but Richard sees him and fights him for it. They pull and jerk the chair back and forth. Chairs are being taken from all over now, back and forth they go, tussles over some. The way to keep your chair is to sit on it. Luke cannot get Richard's chair off him, so he stomps off sulking and gets one of the smaller ones. The small chairs are left until the end. The children less willing to argue for big chairs take what is left, the small chairs.*
>
> *Many times that Ann comes in she sits on Mr Gregg's chair laughing. He has to tell her angrily to move and sit on the floor.*
>
> **Field notes, 1999, Juniors class**

On the last day of term the deputy head promised the year five children that they could sit on chairs at the back of assembly as a treat. When two helpers and a teacher arrived there were no large chairs left and they had to sit in front of us on small chairs. The other teachers made jokes about how they would "be watching them" (in patronising voices) and said, "No talking now or you'll be written in the book," and they laughed at the absurdity of this. The joke needed to be made so as to draw attention to the situation and therefore re-categorise the teachers as teachers who were in the wrong space. The joke was to attribute children's behaviour to the teachers purely because of the space they occupied. The staff were laughing at the absurdity of the positions being switched so as to establish and reinforce the new category amongst themselves. This joking and re-categorisation also highlighted the strictness with which these positions were usually adhered to. The children spent much of their time sitting on the floor, as this was the lowest they can get, indicating their position in the hierarchy.

In assemblies, the classes filed in and out in lines. The children sat directly in order from youngest at the front to eldest at the back. Year six got to sit in the back row on benches; this was a prestigious position, envied and looked forward to by the other children. Children would often try to sit towards the back if they could, especially year five, who often tried to sit, unnoticed, on the benches. Teachers sat around the edge on chairs, not involved in the child hierarchy, showing they were a completely separate group.

> *We come back from the trip to the museum; an older year have used their classroom so there are bigger chairs at their desks. Mary [teacher] says to the infants, "Aren't you lucky, you are going to get to sit on the big chairs for the rest of the day."*
>
> **Field notes, 1999**

Sitting on big chairs is a treat. Chair manufacturers would have us believe that small chairs are made as a convenience for young children, but in fact small chairs carry a heavy significance that far outweighs their comfort.

Access to Space within the School

Powerlessness is embodied through the routine restriction of movement within space. Access to space within the school was controlled by a network of boundaries. There was an eight-foot-high fence round the school (erected while I was there). The children rendered the new fencing and gateway pointless in the first week back at school, as they soon found that they could simply put their arms through the metal gates and press the release button on the other side. The caretaker said to me, "If you want to test something out, just give it to some children." None of the adults, not even the designers, had figured out this possibility. To adults, a barrier is to prevent access; as they understood this, they had not attempted to pass it. Children are far more likely to challenge such boundaries because they have not yet embodied their symbolic significance.

The receptionists controlled the doors and gates to the school; the staff had keys and codes to the doors so that they could move freely around the building. The children watched and memorised the code for the front door and showed off to each other, demonstrating how they could get in and out. These barriers then, to the children, were not simply embodied as barriers as they were meant to be experienced, in the adult way; in addition they were also experienced as something to be resisted.

When children were contained in the school building, group movement from one place to another was done in line with the teacher at the front. Individual movement around the school to the toilet, to other classes, to the headteacher, or to run errands for the teachers was by permission of the teacher. A blue plastic band was supposed to be worn as a sign of having permission to be out of class. These rules were often broken by the children, for instance when somebody stormed out of the class in a temper, or simply left without permission. Sometimes this went unnoticed; at other times the child was reprimanded.

Doorways were specific boundaries, where access was used to exercise power; teachers lined the children up at the door, guarding it until the line was straight and quiet. Only then would they open it. This applied to both going into and going out of class. There were also many invisible doors where children stood: the entrance to the infants' playground was an invisible boundary where juniors would often stand looking across to the other side. This boundary was often crossed and the infants' space was invaded; however the invasion never lasted long as helpers were always on the lookout for such violations. Another invisible door was the one from the juniors' playground through to the car park; it gave access to the main school, the dinner hall, computer room and library. Children were always hovering here; they often took tentative steps over this boundary and sometimes purposely pushed each other across. They found entertaining and inventive ways in which to challenge these boundaries. I saw one boy run along the corridor in school and throw himself onto the floor about five feet away from the swing doors. With his leg out in front, he slid really fast along the floor, kicking the swing door back, and slid the rest of his body through in one smooth motion. Open defiance such as kicking doors open and slamming them shut was a common occurrence, especially when a child was angry with a teacher.

Movement around the school was done in class lines. At the end of break, a bell went, and the children lined up and their teacher came to pick them up. The teacher checked that the line was straight and quiet before moving from the playground into the school. The teacher walked at the front and children were told off if they passed their teacher. The lines, however, never stayed straight; the children chatted and talked as they went along and the lines always had gaps in them, as the children moved along in groups of two, three and four. Children also played at pushing each other out of line or poking, pinching or kicking each other so that they ran out of line.

Movement in space within the school was restricted in that access to certain areas depended on one's status. The staffroom was out of bounds for children and therefore became a space that had on occasion been invaded. In an interview, four boys told me, amongst much laughing and sniggering behind their fingers, about a time when seven of them had invaded the staff room.

> *"Once, right, when we went to get the key for Mr G from the staff room, we saw a tin of biscuits so we ate loads of them [laughing]. We chewed them up and spat some out all over the carpet [hysterical laughing with curling up bodies and holding their stomachs]. Then we left." "Yeah, but then we went back and cleaned it up in case we got found out."*
>
> **Field notes, 1999, Juniors class**

At mealtimes, the children lined up outside in the playground. They were not allowed into the dinner hall until they were quiet enough. They moved in a queue around the dinner hall collecting trays and cutlery and then passed the serving hatches where food was plonked directly onto their trays. Children then had to sit at the empty tables in rotation. If the first table was full you had to sit at the next; however you were not allowed to move on to the second if there was still a space at the first. It was desirable to sit at the later sets of tables if you could, because they were closer to the serving hatches, so if you wanted seconds you would be nearer the beginning of the queue. It was also more desirable simply because getting there meant you had successfully evaded the control over the first area of tables. Many children therefore made a break for it and tried to sit at these tables; they were usually shouted at and sent back to the first three tables, but sometimes they got away with it and were delighted, and encouraged their friends to follow.

> *A boy makes a break for it. "Come on, come on," he says to his friend, whispering loudly and excitedly. He is beckoning with his hand furiously. "She's not looking [meaning the dinner lady], come on." The other child stands hovering from foot to foot, looking back and forth from dinner lady to friend trying to decide whether it's worth the risk. He then quickly runs to the seat, body bent down as if in a military manoeuvre. Hoping not to be seen, he sits down at the furthest table. They wriggle with excitement, heads bent down; smiling and saying "Yes!" under their breaths. They look over to other friends and at the dinner lady. They beckon enthusiastically, saying "Come on." The dinner lady sees them and shouts, "Get back over here," pointing at the first tables. Their faces drop as they are caught. However on their way*

> *back they giggle with each other because they have still triumphed. They did get there for a while, they broke through the boundary.*
> **Field notes, 1999, Juniors class**

The reason they had triumphed was because the purpose was to defeat a restriction, to break through - not necessarily to stay there but just to break a barrier erected by the institution.

Access to Space within the Classroom

In the classrooms there were tables and chairs, trays and cabinets, a carpet for carpet time and a special chair and a whiteboard for the teacher. The juniors and sometimes the infants tried to avoid sitting on the carpet if they could, probably because it was a controlled learning space. Many juniors started off sitting on the classroom floor until they were told individually to move onto the carpet. During carpet time they might also slowly work their way off the carpet onto the floor.

> *At carpet time Janet [infant teacher] says, "Maya, I can't have you there as you won't be able to learn anything. Can you move to a space that you will be able to learn in?" and, "Hands in laps and quiet when learning. Everybody make sure that they are in a space that they can learn."*
> **Field notes, 1999, Infants class**

Once carpet time was over the children usually moved to their desks to work. Among the juniors, this was usually accompanied by much fighting and jostling round the chairs and tables. Once at their tables, the children were supposed to stay at them and do their work. This was resisted in many ingenious ways. The children would get up to borrow rubbers, pencils or sharpeners from other members of the class, usually from the other side of the room, so that they could legitimately walk over there. They would take the long route, chatting on their way. They would blow their noses at the sink, having to return moments later to finish it off. They would ask to go to the toilet over and over again, especially if a friend had just gone. The infants also asked to go to the toilet at the same time as their friends and would immediately go again if they could get away with it. Children would go backwards and forwards to their trays, and infants often went over to the home corner and fiddled for a while, looking busy. These antics took up a large portion of the day. I followed four girls one day, taking note of how much work they actually got done in between these escapades. At the end of the day they each had four sheets of paper on which they had written perhaps a single line, or at most a paragraph. Much more of their school time was spent inventing new ways to resist the institution than on formal learning.

Teachers moved around freely, even though this had the disadvantage that they had to go to the children and sit on the small chairs much of the time, instead of waiting for the children to come to them as teachers did when I was a child. Parents did not go into the juniors' classroom, but they often go into the infants' class, as infants are considered less emotionally capable of dealing with separation. This 'weakness' was also used to control the infants. "I will let the parents in when ...", or "I will not let the parents in until ..."

Access to Space within the Playground

The children were not allowed out of the playground at playtime; if they needed to go to the toilet they had to ask an adult to get permission. The infants had their own playground as they were seen as being more delicate and in need of a separate space to play in or escape to. However they could use the junior's playground at lunchtime and they had it all to themselves in last break as the juniors were still in class. The juniors often hung around the entrance; they tried to break through into the infants' space and sometimes succeeded. When caught, they were abruptly sent back into their own space. The playground had recently been re-designed and redevelopment had started. There was a separate sports area that was used mainly by the boys for football although some of the older girls hung around in there to be near the boys.

The "apartments" was a playhouse split into four rooms. It had only recently been finished. For a long time the site had been cordoned off from the children. When it was opened, the children kept on breaking the boundaries of space within it. A metal barrier had been erected in front of one door to prevent access and to control the flow of children in and out. However the children kept pushing past it; they also climbed through the windows, which was not allowed. The apartments were closed down again a week after they were opened, partly as a form of punishment and partly because the helpers and teachers could not stop the children from breaking the rules. The teachers hoped that if they continuously enforced these rules and closed the building as a punishment when they were broken, the children would eventually stop breaking them. It may have reduced the number of offenders, but I doubt it will have had much effect; the apartments will always be a space of controversy.

There was an area of grass that was cordoned off, as it was not finished; it had a pond in it that was considered dangerous to unsupervised children. A high steel fence barred the grass area. The children constantly broke the rules and leant through the fence to pick stones from the other side to throw at each other. As a result the playground was soon covered in stones.

The children complained about the grass area, as they used to be allowed into the old grass area and they were told this one would be better. Now they were not allowed into the new area as the building of the pond meant that the children could only go in under supervision, and there were not enough staff to provide it. The children were annoyed about this.

A small square memorial garden had been erected in memory of a teacher who had died. It was supposed to be a quiet area of contemplation, but the children used it as a place to hide from helpers while doing things they were not allowed to do. It had a tree in the middle that children were not supposed to climb; to the children, climbing the tree was the main attraction.

Noise Restriction and Resistance to it

Teachers used their voices as a means of control. However, noise levels were also used as a tool for collective resistance by the children. Teachers might use a loud and deep voice to stop the children's noise or a quiet and soft one to make them listen. Janet's voice was a specific indicator to the children as to her mood. She referred to her own voice as her "angry" or "loud" voice. When telling children off, she would shout with a deep voice; when letting them know their behaviour was bad, she would use a shrill, shocked voice; then, as her voice got lighter the children would relax and start to chat again. Ms Smith also used her "cross" voice when the assemblies were noisy; at other times she purposely talked very quietly, so that the children would be lured into being quiet.

As keeping children quiet restricts them, noise from the children indicated that they were excited, and that the adults were losing control. The children always made a loud noise when somebody did something wrong. After an initial moment of quiet the children would burst into noise and movement. The adults had to deal with it quickly before it got out of hand. During the end of year school assembly, year 6 acted out a scene from the Jerry Springer show where fights often broke out. Every time a fight broke out amongst the actors the children in the audience (the whole school) burst into laughter, screaming and shouting. All of the teachers jumped up at this outburst and immediately tried to quieten the children down, shushing and shouting "Quiet!" and making a "calm down" movement with their arms (hands flat, arms outstretched, flapping downwards). It is very important at such a point for the teachers to take control, because if the children carry on getting excited they could lose control altogether, as there are hundreds of children and only a few teachers.

Children use noise control as an inverted tool for resistance. The infants' class and dinner hall were often taken over and disrupted by the children's noise.

> Khalid and John run around the class. When Janet [infant teacher] shouts, "Sit down!" John does. Khalid however carries on running. He is shouting, "I can't talk to you, I can't talk to you," over and over again. Janet counts to three but he carries on. The noise level in the class has shot up; she has to quieten it down by shouting very loud in her "cross" voice. Maya is told to turn round, cross her legs, face Janet and smile. She does not move. After being shouted at again she does. She looks at Janet with her face all screwed up in a frown as if to say, "You can make me sit here but you can't make me like it." The children have got very excited. Two girls tickle each other. They are jumping, squealing, arguing, fighting, laughing - they are very noisy and very lively. Janet shuts the door again, keeping them in. She has to shout at them individually. When we get to the dinner hall, we are half an hour late. It is also very noisy. Zenobi [helper] is there using her whistle, but she is being ignored. The excitement and noise level is far too high to be heard. She has to stand in front of the serving hatch and stop the food being served. However this still has no effect. She whistles again, then Brett comes in and yells in his booming voice. A hush goes through the hall, but very soon after the noise is just as loud again. The children are fighting with the knives and forks; chairs are scraping, tables being banged. I ask Zenobi what she thinks caused it. She says, "As soon as one goes off they all do." This is exactly what seemed to happen in Janet's class. Khalid started it and the others joined in, not listening to the teacher. It was like an incitement to anarchy. The adults appear to be losing control. Zenobi tells me, "I'm blowing my whistle but every time I turn around . . ." They carry on behind her back. The helpers are shouting but the children are not listening. More children than usual are getting away with sitting at the wrong tables. Lunch happens in this loud and haphazard way until the children leave to go out to play. They are simply let out rather than controlled as usual. This means that the noise goes down quicker, order is restored quicker, as the noise dissipates in the playground.
>
> **Field notes, 1999, Infants class**

There was a constant shushing in the school. All of the teachers shushed the children umpteen times a day, in each lesson over and over again, and it had become a habit to many teachers to shush at least once in each sentence, when addressing a group of children. On a trip I saw John, an infant, trying his best to hold his excitement in; his body was jerking around as he tried to stay still and even though he was trying to pinch his lips together with his fingers a stifled noise was coming out through the sides of his mouth.

Again this noise control was subverted as a tool of resistance on the day that a supply teacher was covering in the infants' class. She was reading a story.

> *Bruno starts a quiet shushing sound and the others follow. This gets louder and louder until we cannot hear the supply teacher's voice any more. She stops and says, "No more sound effects." They carry on regardless. She says, "I will remind you that your parents will be coming in to pick you up in twenty minutes and if I have to talk to them you will be in trouble." Bruno says, "You can't talk to mine." Teacher: "Shh." Bruno: "I go to after school club [quietly]."*
>
> **Field notes, 1999, Infants class**

Constituting Control and Resistance

Infants often told juniors what the rules were; the juniors obviously knew these rules but defied them anyway, which was disconcerting for the infants, as they were yet to understand such open ideas of resistance.

> *The infants tell the juniors, "You're not allowed to swing on the trees," "Don't do it or you'll get a pink sheet," "Yeah, or you can't be allowed to play with things in your classroom," "You'll have to stay in." They carry on telling of many ways the juniors might get into trouble. The juniors simply ignore them and later on walk away.*
>
> **Field notes, 1999**

Once something is embodied, it becomes part of the self and harder to see, and it is therefore less likely to be resisted. For example, the juniors had embodied movement around the school in lines; they moved in line without consciously thinking about it. At first infants resisted this control of their bodies, but they did so less as time went on. The control of movement, bodily and within space by the teachers, was therefore gradually internalised, and resistance was reduced. However, it is important to remember that resistance itself is also constituted, that is learned and embodied over time within the fabric of oneself, and juniors who have learnt to control themselves in the manner they have embodied also occasionally try to resist this bodily control. Adults do the same; getting drunk at night-time is a socially acceptable way to break with 'normality' and so resist embodied control.

In schools, power relations, hierarchy and control are exercised, displayed and constituted through spatial constructs such as seating, differential access, restriction of movement and noise. Juniors have embodied some of the control over their movement. Infants have embodied less, and so infants are less adept at performing controlled actions while at the same time chatting with friends.

Infants' resistance is generally more overt than juniors', such as when they refuse to communicate or move. However, they usually follow the teachers' instructions, judge by adults' morals and try to enforce the school rules on others. Resistance is built up over time, in relation to restriction. By the time infants become juniors they have learnt to resist covertly.

Resistance: the Background Theory Applied to Children (A Technical Interlude)

Resistance was largely ignored by ethnographers up until the 1980s, as domination and resistance to it were thought of as relatively fixed ideas. This changed when Foucault and Scott began to write on everyday forms of power and resistance. Scott's (1985) focus on the everyday forms of resistance of "peasants" in his book *Weapons of the Weak* raised the question of how resistance could be defined. Resistance could be found in all areas of life, as power and inequality are an intimate part of all social relations. One of the problems that arose with resistance was to define real resistance; one argument was that a self-serving individual act was not resistance, whilst a principled collective action was.

However Scott argued that everyday forms of resistance and evasion are legitimate forms of resistance, and that peasant resistance takes on a different form from formal hierarchical organised resistance, because peasants need to avoid direct confrontations with authority. Formal organisations have a centre, a leader and an identified structure, whilst peasants' resistance takes the form of such things as foot-dragging, false compliance, pilfering, feigned ignorance, slander and sabotage; it only becomes apparent by analysing their behaviour in more detail. He argues that peasants cannot openly defy and resist the domination of those in power, as this would be dangerous to their livelihood. Furthermore, peasants are always using small advantages to push the boundaries of their relationship, to see what they can get away with, and then 'melting' back into the population for protective cover (Scott, 1985). This angle on resistance is the one from which I am considering children's resistance - they too cannot afford to openly display their resistance; it is too dangerous and they are likely to lose. And so they have invented many ingenious and safe ways to resist without the danger of incrimination.

In *Domination and the Arts of Resistance* (1990) Scott claims that, in public, people play roles that are different to those they play in the private sphere of their own group. He argues that subordinates and those in power have "hidden transcripts", speaking their 'true' feelings when out of earshot of each other. He also acknowledges that it is not clear-cut. It is not the case that people speak their true feelings off-stage and that they always put on a performance on stage. Rather, people have different transcripts for different audiences. He writes of the "hidden transcript within the hidden transcript". Scott argues for "infrapolitics", a strategic form of hidden political action, a form of resistance adapted for those who would be most likely to lose if direct opposition was used. He disputes the ideas of internalised norms of the dominant, which imply that subordinates have simply swallowed the ideas presented to them by the dominant group, believing that subordinates conform only as a result of rewards and punishments that are in place. Even Durkheim, supposedly the theorist of social cohesion, accepted this:

> *This tension in social relations is due, in part, to the fact that the working classes are not really satisfied with the conditions under which they live, but very often accept them only as constrained and forced, since they have not the means to change them.*
>
> **Durkheim, 1964, p. 356**

Gal argues in a hard-hitting criticism of *Domination and the Arts of Resistance* that Scott reduces many different power relations into a simplistic opposition of dominant and subordinate, and argues that such a broad generalisation of forms of power cannot capture cultural differences (Gal, 1995). I agree with Gal that power relations are not a simple case of subordinates versus dominants but a fluid movement of power and resistance, in which the power held by some groups is greater than others. For example, there are pairs of groups such as adults and children, slaves and owners or peasants and nobles where the power difference is vast compared to the less obvious Western division of power between women and men.

The interaction of groups, however, can always be understood in terms of dominance and subordination. One group can also be dominant over one other group and subordinate to a third at the same time, just as we all experience domination and subordination in relation to who we are, and in what relations we are enmeshed. This means that the concept of hidden and public transcripts can only hold true if they are seen as fluid entities that change in relation to one's immediate context.

Howe is another who takes issue with Scott's "binary model of social formations" (Howe, 1998, p. 531), and with the concept of Scott's public and hidden transcripts. Howe argues that Scott neglects the internal power relations between the weak. In his study of unemployed men in Belfast he found that unemployed men, as soon as they gain employment, see men who are still unemployed as scroungers. He criticises Scott for not taking this type of internal conflict into account. I agree with this to the extent that internal conflict is scarce in Scott's work. However, Scott was looking at distinctive power relations where the positions of subordinate and dominant are usually fairly fixed.

A fault with Scott's research is that he chose subjects that fitted his theory, while ignoring those that did not. By contrast, the power relations Howe studied were not fixed. In the context he studied, a person could move from the subordinate into the dominant realm, in other words unemployed to employed. This is not dissimilar, I would argue, to a person moving from childhood to adulthood. This illuminates a different aspect of power relations, as one can criticise and despise one's own group if eventually one expects to progress into the dominant group. Howe argues that disassociating oneself from the subordinate group advances one's own interests - if you can avoid it, you do not want to be associated with a subordinate group. This is very similar to what children do when they enter into the "lying about how old I am" dialogue with their peers.

Kulik also argues against Scott's "hidden transcripts" in his study of Brazilian transgendered prostitutes. The prostitutes use the stereotypical social image of themselves to create 'scandals', whereby a client is embarrassed into paying more by the prostitute threatening to expose the client as wanting to have penetrative sex with him. "They resist by turning the dominant language against members of the dominant group" (Kulik, 1996, p. 7). He claims therefore that the idea of the "hidden transcript" with oppositional values does not hold up. He maintains that this type of resistance depends on stereotypes and oppressive structures to be effective. Furthermore, by making use of this dominant language, he argues that the prostitutes are participating in the maintenance of inequality.

Howe argues that Kulik's and his own example are not unambiguous forms of resistance, and may not even be resistance at all. I would argue that they are using these dominant stereotypes of themselves as tools for resistance. The prostitutes use the dominant's language as a tool to get what they want, to control the situation and therefore as a tool to resist. Scott does address this when he asserts that:

> We get the wrong impression, I think, if we visualise actors perpetually wearing fake smiles and moving with the reluctance of a chain gang. To do so is to see the performance as totally determined from above and to miss the agency of the actor in appropriating the performance for his own ends. What may look from above like the extraction of a required performance can easily look from below like the artful manipulation of deference and flattery to achieve its own ends... In fact, the stereotypes of the dominant are, from this perspective, a resource as well as an oppression to the subordinate.
> **Scott, 1990, p. 34**

In a school, the child who gets to go to the toilet with her friend by using the dominant stereotype of a child being unable to hold her water is an active agent in gaining what she wants, so demonstrating a kind of power. I would argue that we have many transcripts in this context too: children have one for their peers, one for teachers, one for parents and one for other adults. And one may have more than one working at the same time; for example a child may obey the teacher and then "kiss his teeth" at the teacher in purposeful earshot of another child as he passes by.

Abu-Lughod (1990) argues that we should use studies of resistance to diagnose power; and that we tend to get hooked by a romantic idea of resistance because we hope to find failure in oppressive systems. She argues that analysing resistance in this way helps us to understand more about domination and the changing structures of power in society. She argues that Bedouin women use some facets of male domination as a form of resistance which then become a form of power; studying this kind of resistance exposes the complexity of power relations. She suggests that we need to find a way of giving credit to Bedouin women for their resistance instead of "misattributing" forms of politics (that she believes are not there in the first place) or devaluing their practice as pre-political.

Ortner (1995) claims that the problem is "ethnographic refusal", by which she means a failure of "holism or density". As a student of Geertz (1973), the she stresses the importance of thick ethnography (which is whole, complete, dense and descriptive ethnography) while ethnographic refusal points to a thinness (which is lacking in description and density). She argues that this is a reason for ambiguity around resistance. She argues, as does Howe, that the answer to this is further study into the smaller inter-subjective internal relations of subordinate groups such as men and women or parents and children.

After studying the power relations between the inhabitants of the school in my fieldwork, I noticed many similar conflicts between children of different status (for example in a higher or lower class). I suggest that the analysis should be taken further by looking at the internal politics within these relationships. However Ortner rightly argues that the internal politics of subordinates have been "sanitised" or hidden by romanticism. Romanticism causes the deflection of attention to the dominant and subordinate 'good' and 'bad', ignoring those power relations between people within the subordinate group itself. She also asserts that the result of ethnographic refusal is that agency becomes the property of the whole group, the agency of actors within that group becoming lost.

I agree with Scott that it is not the case that subordinates accept what dominants present to them. However, neither is it the case that people hold a completely true or bona fide self, hidden beneath a public façade, as Scott also suggests. As Ortner puts it, "People often do accept the representations which underwrite their own domination. At the same time they also preserve alternative 'authentic' traditions of belief and value which allow them to see through those representations" (Ortner, 1995, p. 182).

I propose that childhood is the place where these ambiguities can be seen most clearly. Toren found that "a discussion of four ethnographic cases where meanings made by children are direct inversions of those made by adults suggests that a systematic study of how children constitute their knowledge of the world is crucial for any analysis of collective relations" (Toren, 1993, p. 461).

Restrictions are placed on childhood because of its socially constructed nature. As childhood is not an inherent thing, children must come to understand what it is, as something "other" than adult or complete/grown up person. And so the child comes to understand that they inhabit a category of people who are not yet complete. Children find themselves in a state of ambiguity. On the one hand they are told that they are naïve, vulnerable and innocent, as the category "childhood" is for those in an "embryonic" state. While, on the other hand, they experience everyday interactions where they are told that they are bad, and therefore deserving of punishment, because those inhabiting the category "childhood" are also in need of being taught how to become a complete person. And in other situations they see "childhood" being represented as a time of romantic resistance, frivolity and acceptable "naughtiness", as is evident in the saying that "Boys will be boys." "Childhood is, simultaneously, the cultural space within which children learn not only what they were but also what they are not and what they will become" (James, 1993). So children may well be agreeing with the adult's concept in the domination of themselves while at the same time holding the concept that domination may be something that is wrong and therefore to be resisted.

4. Power and Resistance

Foucault tells us that power is not a simple binary, that there is one group in direct conflict with another. Rather it is something produced and reproduced through social interaction; it is not something one can own but something that is negotiated, contested or agreed in any given situation. One who holds power in relation to another may, at the same time, be powerless in relation to somebody else.

Power is used in various ways between adults and children, and between children themselves. As power and resistance are everywhere, we need to analyse not only direct confrontation, but also the micro-level of little "digs" here and there. The power of subordinates can itself be used by dominants to maintain power, and children can use adult stereotypes of childhood to their own advantage.

Adults do not have complete power over children. This is evident from the way they attempt to influence children as a way of controlling them, rather than simply commanding them. In the previous chapter I discussed some of the methods of control that are commonly used. However, they do not always work and then discipline and punishment are used to reinforce them.

The Behaviour Policy[1]

Differentiation was evident in the school's behaviour policy, where different ways of being were outlined for children and staff. Juniors frequently complained about the unfairness this caused. They complained that children were not allowed sugar in their drinks and had to be nice and kind to others, while the teachers had sugary tea with biscuits and shouted at the children.

The very presentation of this policy illustrates the different expectations of adults and children. All of the children's codes of conduct for the classroom and the playground tell them how they themselves should behave, whereas the section on teachers' responsibility outlines ways in which the teachers are responsible for guiding and controlling the children. It does not require teachers to show respect for children, to be

---

1   See Appendix Two.

honest, to apologise for mistakes or "move sensibly around the school" as is required of children. The reason is that adults are, because of their age, expected to do some of these things automatically, for instance they are relied on to "move sensibly around the school". As adults they have usually sufficiently assimilated the socially constructed idea of what is normal and what is adult behaviour, whereas children are seen as still learning it. Any adult who breaches this code is assumed to be doing so for a legitimate reason.

The behaviour policy also endorses the restriction children's of movement and noise. "Stay in your seat," says class code of conduct rule 6, "and ask permission to move sensibly and quietly around the room." Such restrictions are to be enforced by the teachers through eye contact, verbal reminders, warnings, ostracism (sitting outside) and punishment. The anti-bullying statement gives the school's definition of bullying: "Preventing somebody from doing what they want or going where they choose, frightening somebody with threats, hurting somebody's feelings by looking at them unkindly." It is interesting that, according to the policy, these very actions are prerequisites for the job of teacher or helper.

Here are some excerpts from *Sanctions used for misbehaviour* (see Appendix Two):

- *Children will be told to stand next to the wall for a specified time for . . .*
- *They may then miss a subsequent playtime . . .*
- *. . . will result in exclusion from the playground for a fixed period of time . . .*
- *Staff use eye contact and verbal reminders or warnings to stop misbehaviour straightaway*
- *. . . move to work at a table alone*
- *. . . spend a lesson of half a day in another classroom or with the headteacher or deputy*
- *parents will be informed and asked to . . . re-inforce the school's disapproval at home*

Many other forms of control and sanctions are discussed elsewhere in this book. The only one I shall mention here is actual physical intervention. When a child (usually an infant) refused to co-operate, they would be picked up or dragged by the arm and put somewhere else. Even though this was not sanctioned by the school, it was frequently done. If a child were to try to use any of these sanctions on another child it would be a clear case of bullying.

Teachers demand politeness from the children while they themselves are often openly rude. A teacher may criticise and demean a child in public; a child who did so would certainly be called a bully.

The behaviour policy and its implementation are full of such contradictions because the school is trying to advocate care, kindness, consideration and freedom for people to work in non-threatening environments, while at the same time its essential mission is simply to control and constrain children against their will. The blame cannot fall onto the teachers or the staff. They are doing their best to be caring and effective teachers. The contradiction is due to the school being an institution for control, part of a wider social structure which requires the subordination and constraint of children so as to uphold the general social order.

Another problem with the behaviour policy is that the terms used have different meanings to the various people that are to enforce it or submit to it. It relies heavily on a common interpretation of broad terms such as "disruptive behaviour", "misbehaviour" and "good behaviour". As the teachers, the staff and the children have different backgrounds, Dockbridge is a multi-cultural school and in any case views on children, caring and behaviour vary so widely - interpretations of such terms can be completely incompatible.

Types of Power and Resistance to it

There are many ways in which one person can hold power or take power from another. Here are a few that are particularly relevant when discussing children in relation to adults.

Knowledge

Children are not allowed full knowledge of the adult world. What information is given is carefully monitored, and in the wider social world you find age restrictions and age segregation everywhere, in cinemas, libraries, Internet sites, exhibitions and even books. Dockbridge sent a letter to the parents to ask permission for children to have sex education classes. (The very fact that a letter had to be sent indicates that sex information is a preserve for adults' control.) Some declined and their children were not allowed to join in the classes with the rest of their year-group. The participants repeatedly recounted stories of the class to the others to demonstrate their superiority - they now had adult knowledge and power that the others did not.

The children would often demonstrate their adult knowledge to their peers by singing dirty versions of songs about sex and kissing.

My boyfriend gave me an apple,
My boyfriend gave me a pear, pear, pear.
My boyfriend gave me a kiss on the lips,
And threw me down the stairs, stairs, stairs.
Under the apple tree,
My boyfriend said to me,
Kiss me, hug me,
Tell me that you love me.
I'm tellin', you're smellin', you went to Batman's wedding.
You kissed his mum and licked his bum and now you're really smellin'.
I'm telling off of you, you dirty kangaroo,
I threw you in the dustbin and turned you into poo.
My name is Coco and I live in a tree,
Selling condoms for 25p.
Big ones, small ones take your pick,
It all depends on the size of your dick.

Field notes, 1999

The more naughty or sexual the rhymes you knew, the more prestige you acquired. However they also had to display a certain amount of wit and facility with rhythm, either to suggest that the singer knew what they were singing about, or perhaps because putting such taboo lyrics to adult formats emphasised their impropriety.

The consumer world of contemporary music, clothes and dance styles is one place where teenagers break out into independence and start to gain adult prestige. To be associated with this world by having knowledge of and taking part in teenage cultural practices gives a younger child power. At Dockbridge, knowing the correct dance movements or the words to pop-songs gave the juniors power. The infants tried to learn but were less adept.

However, regardless of one's age, in one's own circle, the more one knew the more popular one became.

A group of infants are dancing and singing to a small audience including me. Margaritte and her gang come over; they are known to be "up" on the right songs and dances. Elizabeth goes to contemporary dance classes and is looked up to. As soon as they arrive the infants stop dancing and move into the audience, Margaritte and her gang take over the space and start dancing and singing to the same audience. Nothing was said, it was just done, as the older girls are seen as having more knowledge and authority of contemporary music and dance.

Field notes, 1999

Material Objects

Ownership of material objects such as toys, money, labelled clothing and sweets or other food gave higher status. On the school trip to the seaside, the children competed as to who had the most money to spend. In the playground, children brought in sherbet and gave it out to their friends, gaining instant, if temporary, popularity.

> *I am on the carpet with the juniors and Clare comes in to sit next to me. I say hello. She pulls out some sherbet in a straw. The teacher has sat down on his chair and started talking. Clare eats some sherbet. She looks at me and says, "Do you want some?" I say, "I can't, we might get caught." She says, "I'll show you how to do it." She empties the sherbet into her hand and wipes her fingers over her face, licking the sherbet off her palm as it passes her mouth. I am very aware that this defiance of rules is a "buddy thing" if you do it, you are partners in crime. I say again that I daren't. Clare says, "I can give you some and you can go into the toilet if you want to eat it. That's what we sometimes do." I say again that I daren't. I am worried that I may lose the privilege of coming in if I so openly defy the rules, but I am also genuinely scared of the thought of getting caught.*
>
> ***Field notes, 1999***

The giving of sweets is loaded with meaning: it is defying the rules with others therefore identifying and agreeing a common ground; it gains one individual popularity as the owner is wealthy and has something others want; whoever has brought them in has broken the rules, which confers status. It is significant if you refuse sweets that are offered to you, as you are refusing an offer of friendship and denying the value of the sweets. I think I got away with it in the incident described above; I was not seen as being unfriendly, on the one hand because I was genuinely scared and Clare could see that I was, and on the other because I am an adult and am expected not to attach so much value to sweets. I wonder whether this refusal would have been taken very differently had I been a child.

> *"She tried to be popular like Margaritte. If you are not popular and then you bring sweets in they are your friend, but after, when all your sweets are gone, they go and say 'I'm not talking to you' and 'Bring some more sweets in tomorrow'."*
>
> ***Interviews, 1999***

To demonstrate ownership over one's own body is also an attempt to demonstrate power. John, a helper, was giving some children henna tattoos and it became a bit of a craze; everybody wanted one, but John could only do one per playtime. The children therefore started doing 'tattoos' in pen on each other's arms and legs. Nobody had objected when John had taken it upon himself to give tattoos, but when the children did it, it caused a great commotion. Parents came in complaining and the teachers had to ban tattooing altogether and give a warning in assembly. The parents, who saw themselves as owners of their children's bodies, were outraged. This way of claiming one's own body is common to many subordinate groups such as sailors, prisoners, soldiers and teenagers or young adults who not only tattoo but also pierce. At Dockbridge the parents saw it as acceptable when John did the tattooing, as he was an adult; his designs were of a certain acceptable standard.

Popularity

Popularity was the main indicator of power amongst the children as far as they were concerned. Four children I interviewed described how it was 'best' and most powerful to be popular.

"Margaritte, I don't know how she became popular."

"I know how she became popular, she goes round touching the boys bums. That's how you get popular."

"When she's walking down the road, yeah, she does it like this [walks up and down wiggling her bum] and the boys watch. She's popular with the boys. The other people want to be popular with her."

"She has friends and nice clothes that she wears, she has friends that have nice clothes, and muscles. Sometimes they give her money."

"Yeah, I gave her money, she even asked me for money."

I ask Sophie, *"Are you popular?"*

"I'm not popular but I've got friends and that. I'm in between popular and not popular, that's what I am."

Mo: *"I'm not popular, definitely not popular but everybody knows my name in this school."*

"What about you, Jane? Are you popular?"

Jane: "No." Others: "Na, no".

Mo: "She's underneath me".

Sophie: "No she's not underneath you, she's on top of you' [they laugh] If you were to draw it on here." [They start to draw lines on the page where they would be placed in a hierarchy]

All say, "Margaritte goes right up top, yeah, yeah."

"Elizabeth is there because she is brainy and knows the boys and that. Marie is there because of her clothes. [They try to put all of the children in.] Rika's not popular. The boys don't even like her."

"Mark?" they all say.

"Yeah, definitely, right down at the bottom."

"Isaac is at the top." They discuss the boys and where the boys should go.

They continue to rank everybody in their hierarchy of popularity. They are clear on the people that go at the very top and the very bottom but dispute some in the middle and some in relation to others.

Interviews, 1999

It did not pay to be "too feisty" either as this meant you had too much knowledge or popularity and you were assuming the superiority of an adult. Mo, who was not popular, knew much more about sex than the others. Every time she said something that implied knowledge that they did not have they said, "Err, you disgusting." Occasionally therefore Margaritte would play at being the weak and vulnerable one. On one occasion, two of the most popular group decided to go against her. She sat on the tarmac in the playground and started to cry. She kept on checking that the others were around and likely to see her. They did and they became very concerned and guilty about how upset she was. They even started to blame each other in a bid to get the closest to her.

Popularity as power was different in the infants; one was considered popular if one was "nice" or "good", and this was judged mainly by adult criteria - whether one had proper manners or good behaviour for example.

Popularity is so important that many children check before they do something for fear of not getting it right and therefore looking stupid.

Louis is looking around anxious. He has noticed that it's time for seconds but nobody has his or her hand up yet. He wants seconds but is too unsure of himself to dare put his hand up alone. He says out loud, not to anyone in particular, "Why has no one got their hand up?" [for second helpings at dinner time]. He puts his hand up and then back down again as nobody else does. He checks to see how long the queue is, he sees it is short and says to Sarah, "Why has no one got their hand up?" as having somebody else with you means you are less likely to be wrong or a target for others.

Sarah looks checks around and says, "Yes put your hand up", and they do it together. Then Sarah says, "No one else is." [Hands down] "Oh, Mr Wake's class hasn't been." There is much looking around and checking to see why people haven't got their hands up.

Louis checks: "Yes they have." [Hands up]

Sarah: "Yes they have."

Louis: "No." [Hands down]

Sarah: "Yes."

Louis: "Oh yes." [They both put their hands up again, others follow. Louis and Sarah are relieved when they see others put their hands up and finally relax.]

Field notes, 1999, Juniors class

Both Louis and Sarah were worried that they might have their information wrong and they feared retribution and ridicule from their peers. This type of fear of ridicule for getting it wrong was also apparent in the sex education class. The teacher was asking for a show of hands to find out what attributes people thought were important in choosing a friend. Many children checked the rest of the class response before putting their hands up. No hands went up for "good-looking", although many children were looking around at each other for a response. When I saw the written sheets later it became apparent that ten girls had ticked this box but then scribbled it out afterwards when they thought that nobody else had ticked it.

Physical or Mental Ability

Being able to tie one's shoelaces, construct a building, or get the right answers in maths meant that in class you would always have friends sitting next to you. The infants tried to claim recognition by claiming others' achievements as their own - paintings or sculptures for instance.

On the school trip to the seaside, the power relations between the children changed somewhat. Many of the children who usually had "street credibility" in the city were not used to being outdoors. It soon became evident that the able children were becoming popular for the day. Peter, who was usually ignored in class, but was an excellent swimmer and Mary, who could pick up jellyfish, suddenly became the centre of attention. They shone in their new roles. The children who were usually the most popular simply seemed to take on a less prominent role for the day.

Stickers, headteacher's awards and smiley faces were given for being a 'good' child. They were designed for adults to use as a means to control. Here is an excerpt from *Behavioural Rules and Sanctions*:

For particularly good or noticeably improved behaviour:
- A child's name will be written on the class board or in a class book
- Parents will be informed verbally
- Their name will be written in the special Thursday assembly book, read out and they will receive a headteacher's award
- Any child receiving 3 gold stickers will take home a certificate from the headteacher

Class teachers also set up their own reward system of ticks, stars, stickers, smiley faces or certificates.

Gaining such awards made you popular with the teachers and your parents, which could on occasion be both useful and desirable. However, they did not necessarily make you popular with your peers.

Power Withheld and Bestowed as Control

Within the school adults bestowed or withheld small amounts of power and this was used as a way of encouraging the children to conform. In the infants' class the children were given turns at being leader. Being leader meant that, for the day, one was allowed to go in the front of lines, to choose activities first and pick a friend to take the register back to reception with you. You were also expected to show the rest of the class how to behave and you got to take the special book and toy home for the night. Being leader made you popular as you had power to choose, bestow privileges such as going to the office with you, or lining up first.

Maya: "When I'm the leader I'm going to choose Ben as my helper." [She says this twice as nobody responded the first time. Earlier she had said she would choose both Ben and Marge. However Maya and Marge have just fallen out.]

Marge: "I'm going to choose Maya." [Even though Maya hasn't chosen her].

Maya looks over at Marge as she is surprised at this, she then smiles and says, "I'm going to choose both of you." Maya had left Marge out, Marge got Maya to make up indirectly, by using the future power of when she is going to be leader.

Field notes, 1999, Infants class

The drawback of being leader was that, if you did not conform and were not on best behaviour "showing the others how to behave"; your leader status was threatened or taken away altogether. This threat was used by the teacher to control the leader and therefore became another mechanism for controlling the class.

Janet [a teacher]: "Karl would you like to be the leader, please, as Brian is not ready at all?" "Karl go and line up at the door." Brian throws his head into his arms and cries out very loudly. Once the line is made he looks across at Janet, sobs and cries out across the room.

Janet: "Brian, do you think you can be sensible today? Then I might give you another chance."

Brian nods his head. She says, "Karl we are going to give Brian another chance to show us how sensible he can be as our leader." [This is not directed at Karl but at the whole class.] Brian jumps up and goes to the front of the line. The helper says, when he passes her, "... and if you stop crying, that is," wagging her finger in his face. Even though it is called "in front of the line" it is still behind Janet. Brian is attentive throughout assembly. As we leave the hall for playtime Brian starts crying again, as he wasn't put in the front of the line. Janet says, "Well, we had to get out quickly as we are missing play." I ask Brian why he cried. He said because he "thought Janet had taken the leader off him again because he didn't come out first like leaders do."

Field notes, 1999

Years 5 and 6 were given power by the Rangers system - Rangers exercised control over others and their games. If the Rangers' job was not done in the way expected by the school, this power was threatened and sometimes withdrawn. This situation can be likened to the theory of the creation of the middle classes. A section of the "working class" were given privilege by the "ruling class" so as to divide them from the "masses" and create a "middle class". This division gave the "ruling class" more control.

The formula of "divide and conquer", and the controlling of bestowed privileges to keep a tight hold over overall power, are both used in the education system.

In the Rangers' meeting, where all of the Rangers meet with the deputy head to discuss problems and future plans, the Rangers divulged to teachers how children were resisting the school rules in the playground, thereby acting as informers to gain privilege. This information gave the teachers insight that they could use for further control.

Another privilege for the juniors was to be sent down to the reception class for the afternoon. Permission was usually granted as a reward. The children liked this as they got out of doing schoolwork. In return they had to show the younger ones how to behave 'sensibly' and to conform. If the juniors themselves did not conform correctly, they would be sent back to their classes and lose their privilege. This was therefore an effective tool for controlling not only the juniors but also the infants.

Abu is running around in the toilet. Janet tells people not to look at him. She does the "hands on head" routine. We do it but Abu runs around making noises. Abu is making a farce of the authority and the others like it. They watch him shocked but excited. Janet threatens to put people's names on the board; Abu makes more noise. He is getting bolder each time Janet makes a new threat. Janet is now threatening the others. She has given up on Abu; it is about keeping the rest of the class in order now. Abu does threaten her control over the class as the others are getting more lively. However they are also aware of Janet's authority and position in relation to Abu's. The atmosphere is very tense. This seems to keep them at bay.

Janet says that everybody should ignore Abu, and nobody is to speak to him at all. She counts each child in, putting her hand firmly on their head as they walk by and says she expects complete silence. If anyone talks, their name goes on the board. We go in and sit on the carpet.

Janet asks Abu if he is coming in. He shakes his head. Janet says, "Come in when you are ready to come in." Two minutes later Abu comes in and makes a noise. Mira says, "Look at Abu." Janet writes Mira's name on the board. She tells Abu to sit on the carpet and says "Good boy" when he does. I think he does this because he realises he has no backing from the others. Karl says something; his name goes on the board. The class is silent as Janet reads a story, apart from Abu who is saying "rip" [or something that sounds like that]. He says it louder and louder, over and over. Other children tell him, "shhh." Janet says, "Ignore him." Abu is not shouting it, but as the class is silent, it does sound loud. Isaac [one of the older boys from Mr G's class that has come in to help the younger ones learn how to behave] smiles at me as Abu gets louder, as if to say this is outrageous but hilarious; he likes it. Isaac is a junior who is usually disruptive in his class and is always being told off for it. However he has never been as defiant as Abu is being now. Isaac is suddenly very well behaved - this is totally out of character for him. Janet says "Flowers" in the story loudly. Abu shouts "Flowers" and "Bum, bum" really loud. Abu gets louder and more frequent. Janet says to Isaac, "Do you want to take Abu out if he carries on?" Isaac looks at his friend, smiling as if to say, "You must be joking." He doesn't answer Janet. Abu puts his head in his arm, shaking his head. Isaac doesn't move. Abu stops making the noise.

Field notes, 1999

Isaac was enjoying Abu's defiance of authority, but he appeared to be frozen with fear and not to know what to do. In his own class he would most likely have joined in. He was aware of his position as 'model child' and pseudo-authority and worried about the consequences of any action he might take himself. Though he clearly did not want to be given the job of dealing with Abu, he did not refuse to do so but simply stayed silent, hoping the request would not be repeated.

The infants had also constituted the idea that one is better if one acts like a junior, in the same way as in the western capitalist world people believe that it is better to be like the middle class than the working class. This means that when a junior acts in the way that the teachers have imposed, the infant constitutes this pseudo-junior behaviour as the way a junior really is.

Material Objects

Material objects were often confiscated. Every day when the children came into school, the first thing the juniors had to do was to empty their pockets of money, toys, bus passes and food, and hand everything over to the teacher. It was given back at the end of the day. This is very similar to the stripping of prisoners of their personal identity in order to take away their power in prison. School uniform, like prison uniform, also strips a child of a personal identity or expression of self. Luckily there is no uniform at Dockbridge. Scott (1985) points out that euphemisms are used to mask negative actions, such as restricting somebody in a straitjacket being called "calming them down". In school, confiscating your belongings in order to exercise control is called "looking after it for you".

Parents sometimes exercise power over their children by making them wear clothes they do not like to school. However this can be resisted. Every morning Margaritte brought her clothes to school in a bag. In the toilets she took off the dowdy blue skirt her mum sent her in and changed into her short leather pants and glittery top. In the afternoon she changed back into the dowdy skirt before going home.

Another way for children to resist is by defying the teacher's ownership of school materials.

> *Margaritte has two pieces of paper. Mr Grain [a junior teacher] comes and takes one back, she whispers, "Be selfish then." Later she goes over to his desk and steals another, smiling over at me. She goes back and takes another five and shoves them behind the shelf. Mr Grain sees and tells her to go outside. She does, but a few minutes later the door opens and her hand comes in, reaches over his desk and takes yet more paper out.*
>
> **Field notes, 1999, Juniors**

Physical or Mental Ability

Adults cannot easily exercise control by the use of a child's physical or mental ability, as this is determined by the child's individual achievement. However, ability can be turned into a tool to control through the use of competition. Creating competition causes achievement to become a means of proving oneself to others, rather than a form of power for oneself.

The infants tended to desire adult approval, whereas the juniors tended to desire their peers' approval. John and Peter (infants) were sitting at the construction table. Peter had built an elaborate construction. John had not built anything but noticed that Peter had:

John: "Peter is that for me?"

Peter: "What?"

John: "Is that for me, can you make it for me please?"

Peter: "No."

John: "Peter can you make it for me?" [He comes over and sits on Peter's chair as Peter is standing up next to it]

John: "Can I show it, Peter?" [Meaning show it to his teacher as his]

Peter: "No."

John goes over to his own chair picking up some of his stuff. "I'll help you Peter, I'll make yours the best one." He starts building some sticklebricks onto the edge of Peter's model. Peter picks it up and walks away with it. John's added bits fall off. Peter shows the model to his teacher who says, "Yes, that's good. Put it on the table."

John then goes over to Janet, shouting, "Janet, Janet look, look," tapping her on the arm and pointing to Peter's model. He is claiming it as his. Janet assumes it is both of theirs and says, "Yes, John, that's very good."

Field notes, 1999, Infants class

John was desperately trying to get Janet's approval by pretending he was physically adept like Peter.

The class was also openly controlled by the use of competitiveness, as one is popular if one is a winner.

Teacher: "Let's show Bruce we are the quietest class in the school."

"If we don't hurry up Luke's class will beat us into dinner."

Field notes, 1999

On the school trip to the seaside, even though a toilet was working and available on the coach, the teachers told the children that it was broken. If they wanted to go to the toilet or be sick, they would have to use a small bucket. This of course was embarrassing for the children, as they did not want to perform in front of their friends - they would be laughed at and their popularity would go right down. The teachers agreed on this deception because they wanted to stop the children spending lots of time going to the toilet and to keep them all seated and therefore controlled. This was very effective. On a one-and-a-half to two-hour journey, out of approximately ninety children, ranging from age 4-10, only one four-year-old boy used the bucket. The rest hung on until we got there.

Popularity and Resistance to Authority

Doing 'bad' things that are against the moral or formal rules of the school was seen as brave. Bravado is portrayed as heroic in the media all around us. There are images of subordinate heroes who fight and triumph over evil dominant systems, from Brer Rabbit who outwits the bad and selfish Brer Fox, to the working-class hero who fights his righteous way through a battleground of vicious bureaucracy, as in films like *Michael Collins* and *Braveheart*. Dennis the Menace and Minnie the Minx in the *Beano* appeal to children because they are constantly resisting domination by teachers and adults; the weak triumph over the strong. Often, in the bigger scheme of things, the subordinate appears to lose. However it is clear that we are on the side and in agreement with the righteous oppressed and not the oppressor, the "goody" not the "baddy". It is interesting that these images of heroes are provided by adults; I would suggest that this is because they themselves were children (the subordinates) once and they too value resistance.

The child who fights the restrictions of the institutional system can become popular. This was more apparent with the juniors than the infants, probably because the infants had not yet understood the hypocrisy of the institutional system as well as the juniors had.

Sajeed: "Isn't it that Sylvia, she stole something from the shop?"

Laya: "She never stole nothing."

Sajeed: "Yeah, she did, she stole this chocolate bar from the shop."

Laya: "Yeah, she said she did but I was with her when she bought it."

Sajeed: "No, she stole it."

Laya: "No she never. I was with her, from the cash and carry. What chocolate was it?"

Sajeed: "It was this little one."

Laya: "No, I was with her when she bought that, she didn't steal it. She told me 'I want to be popular and I want to get something and tell everybody I stole it, to be popular,' but she didn't steal it she bought it."

Sajeed: "I admit that I stole something, I admit that I did."

Alice: "It's like being naughty or like you're on drugs like Michael Jackson or something."

Joanna: "So is being popular really important?"

All: "YES! YES!"

Alice: "It's important for your reputation."

Joanna: "So what are different ways of getting popular?"

Laya: *"You might steal something, being naughty, silly, eat chewing gum in school."*
Interview, 1999, juniors class

However, this is not always the case, as children who make themselves conspicuous by being too different from the others can also become isolated.[2] Fighting the system can be dodgy too; there is a thin line between heroic and criminal, and anybody who crosses it loses popularity. This is especially so if the criminal act is committed against another child.

There is, of course, a class element that runs through all this; while the working-class children bang against the system and are frequently reprimanded, the middle-class children tend to be a bit annoyed at the waste of time these escapades cause. "Once the working-class boy begins to differentiate himself from school authority there is a powerful cultural charge behind him to complete the process" (Willis 1977, p. 74). As Willis points out this class-inspired differentiation continually widens the gap between the working class boy and 'acceptable' middle-class society. He becomes increasingly categorised as a "worker" rather than a "thinker" and this will still be the case when he begins to take part in adult society.

The infants had fewer romantic stories than the juniors to tell about children getting the better of adults - they have had less experience. However a charge of excitement and fidgeting swept through the classroom when somebody did decide to defy the teacher. In the leavers' assembly, when a Jerry Springer skit was performed by the juniors, the whole school, infants and all, chanted and egged the actors on, as this kind of anarchistic behaviour, even when acted out, was not usually allowed in school. When a fight scene broke out the children started jumping, screaming and cheering, while the teachers hovered, unsure whether to step in. At this point the headteacher had to threaten to send some children out, even though she didn't really like the parents to hear her doing so.

Just as the adults use children's forms of power to control them, children manipulate the adult stereotypes of "child" to get their own way. As Scott argues, it is possible for people to reinforce their own stereotypes

---

2 ". . . an excess of individuality, or its inappropriate cultural expression, may confer outsiderhood, leading to the stigma of 'exclusion from the crowd'. The skill lies in knowing how, when and where to reveal it." (James, 1993, p. 151).

to their own advantage. Children sometimes use crying to get a teacher's attention; this is working from the constructed idea of child as vulnerable, while at the same time reinforcing the adult's idea of the child as vulnerable, sensitive and weak.

In the adult world, subordinates use many techniques of resistance to diminish the power of dominants, including attacks on dominants' property and character assassination. There was much evidence of this in the school; children drew on desks, blackboards and wall maps and stuck chewing gum on the floor or under desks. At lunchtime, when getting water, children would purposely pour water onto the water trolley so as to cause a mess, afterwards boasting, "I poured four cupfuls on there." There was a constant slandering of teachers and helpers amongst the children and also to parents. One question I was frequently asked when I was conducting group interviews was, "Can we diss the teachers?" I was told many incriminating things about teachers that were probably not true. The children were very keen for me to expose their allegations to "the newspapers" and "get the school closed down." I doubt if they would have been so forthcoming if there was any chance of this actually happening. However some of these allegations had been reported to the headteacher, so they may not all have been made up.

Power

Power does not persist from one situation to another. An in-depth knowledge of Barbie dolls may be power among four-year-olds, whereas such interest in Barbies would be open to ridicule among ten-year-olds, and would reduce any source of power.

A child may hold power over an adult in an isolated incident, for instance by using an adult construct to get away with something. She may say sorry as she purposely breaks a rule, knowing that she is not sorry but that "sorry" is the accepted appropriate response. Or she may embarrass her male teacher by referring to her period when she asks to go to the toilet, knowing that it will embarrass him so much that he will just say, "Yes, go," rather than get into a discussion about it. That child is nevertheless still subordinate to the larger institution that imprisons her, and also to the wider social structure that houses the institution. The child therefore can never unambiguously hold power over an adult. As Willis (1977) points out, one cannot study isolated incidents or isolated institutions but must look at the wider social context.

Children are active agents who resist within a restrictive environment, which is legitimised by the wider social structure. Direct confrontation may make sense in the negotiation of power with one's peers, as one stands a chance of proving a higher status and therefore having power, but the child is also in the process of constituting the politics of power, in that direct confrontation is not necessarily the most effective means of resistance when dealing with those in a much more legitimised and powerful position than oneself. This means that resistance to adult's power will often be covert and difficult to recognise.

Power and resistance are not simple oppositions but complex networks, as you see when you look at the detail of various forms of power use and resistance. I found that knowledge, material objects, popularity, physical and mental ability were tools for holding power over others. Subordinates' forms of power can be subverted by dominants into power over them (for example knowledge, popularity), whilst dominants' stereotypes (for example children are vulnerable and weak) can be subverted by subordinates into resistance, and therefore a form of power. Furthermore what is used as power over a person may also be used by that person to hold power over another. For instance a form of bullying such as ridicule that is used by a teacher can then be used by the victim to bully a child younger than himself. In addition, while people may hold power in one context they may still be subordinate to the wider social context of institutional power.

Infants are in the process of learning through restrictions and resistance how to manipulate and manage power, while juniors, as a result of their history and experience are more adept at this. However, infants are also skilful in inventing new creative forms of manipulation. As Toren argues:

> *In no case can the adults [or juniors] be said to "know better" than the children [or infants], even if they may be said to "know different" and to "know more". Moreover, in each case, what the child [or infant] knows remains an integral (if implicit or even denied) part of the adult's [or junior's] concept.*
>
> **Toren, 1993, p. 473**

Politics and Power in Relation to Children

> *Power is employed and exercised through a net-like organisation. And not only do individuals circulate between its threads; they are always in the position of simultaneously undergoing and exercising this power.*
>
> **Foucault, 1976, p. 234**

Everyday repression is as hard to identify, as is everyday resistance - they both function as inconspicuously as possible. Feminists were reluctant to accept Foucault's theory of power being everywhere because binary models were useful for pinpointing oppression from dominant groups. However subordinates can hold and use power as active agents even within an oppressive system. They can be seen as active agents who play a part, rather than passive victims. When subordinates use the dominant ideology itself to resist, this is not a case of denying the oppressiveness of the system but rather an example of the oppressed person's inventiveness in finding ways to hold power within that system.

To separate adulthood from childhood by making children a politically victimised minority group, or to look at childhood as a separate culture, is dubious (see James, Jenks and Prout, 1998). The notion of a separate autonomous "children's world" as in Opie and Opie's study of children's cultures (1959) is a typical western capitalist illusion. Adulthood and childhood are two parts of one political whole and cannot be studied in isolation, as doing so neglects the inter-subjective relations between adults and children. As the negotiation of power relations takes place in inter-subjective relations with others, it is possible that the constitution of subjectivity incorporates a political process. The categories of childhood and adulthood are an intrinsic part of a wider politically social context. This context, therefore, must play a part in the constitution of a person's subjectivity through interactive relations.

Political powerlessness is imposed upon children by adults, who usually hold power. Powerlessness in childhood becomes a web of restriction; the reason given for imposing this powerlessness is protection and control. This protection and control also applies to other groups that are ambiguously placed in the same category of "childhood" even though they are not children, such as people who have supposedly regressed, such as those labelled as "mentally ill" or those who have supposedly never "grown up" and are categorised as "retarded". As Goode argues, since childhood is a socially constructed category, children can pass biologically through childhood without ever being given the title child, whilst others can be placed in the category while being biologically adult (Goode, 1986). This powerlessness is a part of the category "childhood", and is therefore ascribed to those who are in it. It does not necessarily follow, however, that those people are actually powerless in practical terms. In fact they find ways to negotiate with authority despite the powerlessness generally imposed upon them.

5. Food for Thought

Adult-child power relations are constituted, learned and understood through the embodied restriction of movement within space and control of various elements of power, such as noise, knowledge, and access to material objects, and manipulative use of popularity and status attached to physical or mental ability. Children interact with both adults and other children. They are therefore not merely products but also producers of society.

It is popularity with their peers that plays the most important role in children's own construction of the ideas of children and childhood. As popularity is a form of power and one desires power, one unconsciously and consciously conforms to what will make one popular. This reinforces the constitution of ideal personhood that society has dictated. However this ideal is principally for display, so even when one conforms in order to become powerful, one does not necessarily believe that one is expressing one's true identity. For example, one may pretend to know all of the dance moves to a song when in public, even though one knows that this is not actually so.

This brings us back to Scott's idea of public and hidden transcripts. I maintain that people do have public and hidden transcripts; however, as I have shown, there will be many of them and they will change in relation to one's audience at any given time. Juniors converse with each other in very short, sharp sentences when they do not want adults to understand them. In my interviews I was told that "teachers tell you not to tell your parents" about specific incidents. This directly teaches the idea of separate transcripts for separate audiences. Furthermore, teachers have higher expectations of the juniors and so are stricter with their techniques of control, forcing them to devise more subtle styles of resistance, whereas the infants are seen as the ones who do not understand yet and are therefore allowed to get away with more confrontation. As Scott also points out, dominants have their hidden transcripts too; teachers hide their privileges, such as teachers' biscuits in the staff room, and they creep away secretly to smoke cigarettes on school trips.

It is important to remember the idea of "children as resisters"; rebellion and resistance are also being constituted. Children come to resist as a response to restrictions in their daily lives and their growing awareness of the paradox of the school system. Infants show signs of learning covert resistance over time. During the transition from infants to juniors, they are always in the process of understanding and constituting power and control, and working out how to manipulate and resist them in less obvious and incriminating ways. The juniors' resistance therefore is more similar to that observed by Scott among adult Malaysian "peasants", involving such techniques as character assassination, vandalism, feigned ignorance and foot-dragging.

It is also apparent that, although most children find resistance "cool" and "wicked", some children resist more than others do. Age and class influence how much a child conforms or resists, as do cultural background and gender. A child may also have been exposed to political influences such as notions of democracy and equality, either in interactions with adults at home and through the media, which will play a part in how they come to resist.

Social Change and Children's Part in it

Children's resistance to adult authority or domination can be likened to the everyday forms of resistance practiced by "peasants".[1]

The acts of defiance in which children take part at school and at home have a political effect on the larger issue of "childhood". I do not suggest that it is a conscious political collective movement, but rather an individual process of resistance. The child who recognises a restriction, resists it and defies it may not be aiming to break down a dominant system, but is simply defying a rule on a personal level.[2]

The concept of childhood is slowly breaking down in Western society. There are constant changes in the law needed to cope with children who do

---

1 "It is perfectly legitimate even important to distinguish between various levels and forms of resistance; formal-informal, individual-collective, public-anonymous, those that challenge the system of domination - those that aim at marginal gains" (Scott, 1985, p. 299).

2 Scott argues by use of simile that: "Just as millions of anthozoan polyps create, willy-nilly, a coral reef, so do the multiple acts of peasant insubordination and evasion create political and economic barrier reefs of their own. And whenever the ship of state runs aground on such reefs, attention is usually directed to the shipwreck itself and not to the vast aggregation of petty acts that made it possible. For these reasons alone, it seems important to understand this quiet and anonymous welter of peasant action" (Scott, 1985, p. xvii)

not fit into the category "child", such as child criminals, and an attempt is being made to hold such children accountable for their actions. This moves us away from the idea of 'childhood innocence' according to which children who committed crimes were thought not to know any better. When children are held responsible for their actions they are seen as "knowing better". The laws governing their behaviour not only change to control them, but change to become more like those governing adult's behaviour. The category "child" is therefore shrinking as younger and younger people no longer fit into it.

Social change happens over time because people's ideas of the "ideal person" change. Many minor inter-subjective encounters will gradually change people's ideas. Even though children are not listened to directly, indirectly they affect social change. Each time an adult hears a child swear, as a resistance to a prohibition, it slowly - perhaps over decades - becomes more acceptable to the adult's ears. When I was doing my research, juniors' persistence in bringing sugary drinks into school against the rules was eventually accepted by the teachers; they simply gave up trying to enforce the rules; the sugary drinks thus started to become acceptable. When the brick play-boat in the school playground was first built, the children were strictly forbidden to sit on the high wall which made up one side. As the children always disregarded this rule, many adults now ignore it, as they don't want to keep repeating themselves. As Zenobi (a helper) said, "They've got to do something to enjoy themselves - you can't always be telling them off."

Power relations are points of negotiation. Through punishments, discipline and control, adults negotiate and sometimes impose their idea of what it is to be a person. Through interactions such as resistance to adults' ideas, both explicitly and implicitly, children negotiate, accept or refuse this. Through these inter-subjective encounters, power relations and ideas of personhood are in constant negotiation and change. We hear the concerns of adults frequently reiterated on the news - how the young people of today are "getting worse", and "older earlier", or how they are "old beyond their years". Every small movement a child makes, every interaction or negotiation that happens between adult and a child changes the face of the category "childhood". Children play an active role in social change. It is therefore vital to the understanding of social change that children's understandings of the world and participation in it are considered just as seriously as those of adults. However, we must remember that researchers who divulge children's forms of resistance may inform those in dominant positions, thereby giving them insights and additional power.

As the concept of "childhood" is breaking down, children are being increasingly held responsible for their actions. The more children are held responsible, the more rights to the adult world they must gain. I suggest that this is why we have a rise in the number of schoolchildren being caught up in the mental health system. As children are seen as more responsible, more whole, then their behaviour (too much movement, noise, flexibility or creativity) is increasingly been categorised as abnormal and to be prevented. Ten per cent of children in American schools are now being drugged by Ritalin to help them conform to our irrational, unnatural, quiet, still, well-behaved, monotonous society. Being a child is no longer a good enough excuse for being alive, zestful or rebellious; as semi-persons, children may be on the road to 'madness' and are thought to need psychiatric drugs to turn them back.

School and Education - Learning Capitalism

Education (as it presently exists in the West) is about growing children into "whole human beings". It is about educating and socialising them into becoming civilised (like us). This is absurd. The reality is that young people are whole human beings already. They have empathy and ideas and creativity that we have lost touch with. Because their ways are so different from ours, we think they need to learn our ways. This is fundamentally wrong. They do not need educating into our capitalist, oppressive way of doing things. We need to learn from them. Educating children into being "something better" is both patronising and oppressive.

Having knowledge and information is not synonymous with clear thinking. Educated people are not more intelligent than uneducated ones. A grasp on reality does not require education. It may require a lack of education as we know it. The children who are best at fighting oppression and showing that they remember how their lives ought to be - full of freedom, love and respect - are usually those "playing truant" and getting little education. They are the ones refusing to conform to an irrational society. Philosophical thinking and theory can help to inform an already assimilated adult and encourage flexible thinking. Children are able to be flexibly intelligent before this assimilation. Since children are less assimilated into capitalist conformity, they have a clearer grasp on reality. Not knowing how to cross a road because the society one lives in has not taken into account that a young one may wish to move around freely or not being able to add a list of numbers does not mean one thinks or knows less.[3]

The Way Forward

Schools are oppressive institutions, no matter how hard the people inside them are trying to reform and improve them. The job of schools is to 'educate' or train children into conformity to an irrational capitalist society where people are only valuable if they produce profit.

Rational education systems or information centres would be so different from the ones we have now that there is no point in tinkering with what we have. Trying to reform an oppressive system in a piecemeal way is useless.

Mass education, whether in schools or in the mental health system, is a device to teach and reproduce class systems. It is a tool to teach people their place in life and encourage them to try to 'better' themselves. It is built upon the assumption that young human beings are not good enough as they are. The education system is an institution of social control that reinforces the status quo. This system effectively constitutes the idea of person as a well-educated, well-behaved, quiet, nice, co-operative human producer of profit for the capitalist system. This status quo of normality and conformity is also supported by a class system, where the idea is reinforced by the middle-class preoccupation with the idea that education makes you into a 'better' person.

If we wish to change society and allow the growth of new, fresh, flexible, intelligent, creative and inventive thinking which will advance our societies, then we must stop trying to confine everybody into the same narrow boxes. We must abolish the education system as we know it, along with the class system, and we must begin by ending the oppression of young people.

---

3   As Toren points out "In no case can the adults be said to 'know better' than the children, even if they may be said to 'know different' and to 'know more' " (Toren, 1993, p. 473).

Afterword: The Wider Social Structure/Mental Health System

Through the writing of this book I have come across many other groups of human beings who seem to be placed under the category of "child" without actually being a child. As mentioned earlier, Goode demonstrates how "retarded" people can, even though are biologically adult, still inhabit the category of child, in that they are considered to have never grown up. This placing of people who are biologically adult in the category of childhood also applies to people who have been labelled as "mentally ill". They are considered to be people who, because of their illness, have become like children or at least need to be treated and taught in the same manner as children to learn to become whole again. The sanctions and behavioural type "therapy" are all similar. The only exception there might be are those who are considered to be "criminally insane". These people inhabit a category of "bad", "evil" or even non-human. Children who have committed murder (which does not fit the category of "child" at all) are thrust out of the category of child and also put into the category of "bad", "evil" or non-human. Hence in the Jamie Bulgar case where two ten-year-old boys killed Jamie a two-year-old boy, the children were labelled as "devils".

Significance of the Wider Social Structure

In the wider social structure, schools are seen as a gateway to the outside adult world, a place where children learn and become 'civilised', that is to say culturally and socially adept. Schools are institutions of social control, a complex network of control exercised through their hierarchical and disciplinary structure to ensure that children conform. The marginalisation of children entails economic, social and political restrictions and serves as a backdrop to the school system of control. Because children have no economic value, this legitimises the control, which is anyway seen as vital to the harmony of the social system as a whole. If children do not conform then the local authority will take over and then the courts or the health service, until either they eventually conform or are removed from society and referred back to the system of institutional control, for example borstal, prison or, in the case of people who have passed through "childhood" and still not conformed appropriately, the mental health system.

The mental health system is a gateway through which one who is temporarily labelled as not "normal" (that is, not culturally or socially adept) can enter "ill" and re-emerge as a "whole" human being. This is done with the aid of mind-altering drugs, electric shock treatment, isolation and other forms of physical abuse. Otherwise a mental hospital may be the end of the line, the rubbish tip for those people who are seen as being permanently 'subnormal'. This is a very effective institution of social control - it 'cures' some and deters others.

The marginalisation of people labelled mentally ill ensures that economic, social and political restrictions are placed on them. As with children, this serves as a backdrop to the mental health system of control. People labelled as mentally ill have no economic value and as with children this reinforces and condones their mistreatment as legitimate as it upholds the harmony of the social system.

The Conforming Process

Many of the restrictions placed on children that have been discussed in this book mirror those in the mental health system. Many ways of making people conform have been thought up for both children and people labelled as having mental health problems. They are unsurprisingly similar.

Foucault shows that definitions of madness have varied over time. Since the 18th century, when societies first defined the difference between normal and abnormal, they have used these definitions to govern behaviour.

Samuel Tuke, an 18th century Quaker, believed that the mad were like children who must be disciplined and raised, learning respect for authority and religion. They were to learn this through chores and activities, timetables and regulation. Tuke watched and monitored the patients and doled out punishments and rewards for "proper" behaviour. At that time, everyday behaviour was being put under surveillance and scrutiny.

The Panopticon designed by Jeremy Bentham (1748-1832) is a tower from which warder, doctor, teacher or foreman can spy on and penetrate behaviour. It locates bodies in space, in relation to each other. The subjects under surveillance never know quite when they are being watched and so effectively police themselves.

Horrocks and Jevtic, 1999, p. 118

Afterword

Today people labelled as having mental health problems, like children, are put into institutions where they are supposed to learn something - about the world, the way things are "supposed to be", the way one is "supposed" to act. They are encouraged, coerced, threatened, forced and blackmailed into taking part in "educational" activities or activities that will promote "normal", "sociable" behaviour. Resistance takes the everyday form because direct defiance or confrontation can lead to severe punishment, just as it does with children.

Resistance is not seen as a political statement but as uncooperative behaviour. Only acceptance of the power system and its terms will get patients classified as normal, and thus earn their release (Fillingham, 1993, p. 147).

As excessive noise or movement may result in a person being sectioned, people in the "community houses" or rehabilitation wards are often quiet and subdued. However, people who have recently been sectioned, and are therefore in the acute wards, frequently fight the institution. Physical force, isolation and drugging are used to stop them. Most mental health hospitals are made up of a series of wards that a person moves through in relation to how well-behaved they are. People who have been sectioned for inappropriate behaviour are originally admitted to the acute wards, where most are not allowed out at all; they are continually observed and monitored, heavily drugged, and physically, mentally and emotionally controlled. Once they have reached a particular level of subdued behaviour, they are gradually given rewards, such as permission to have their own cigarettes or small amounts of freedom. The doctors in the reviews, which take place weekly or monthly, grant these privileges. Reviews are anxious times for inmates; they are tests and evaluations where staff and workers report on you and your behaviour to the doctor. If your behaviour is approved, you may move to the rehabilitation wards, where you are expected to partake in a certain number of activities. (Some people do go into the acute wards and return directly into the community with their drugs, but they are often sectioned again at a later date.) Some resist taking part in these activities, but if you do not go to a enough activities each week, it will go down in your notes, and in your review you will be described as uninterested or non-compliant, for example. If you comply and behave in the right, subservient way, you may eventually be allowed to move to a community house. People who have been in the mental health system for five years or more are very keen to be placed in community houses, as there they generally have more freedom to come and go.

Today's madhouses are a series of gradated wards, through which the inmate can move only by good, appropriate, sane behaviour, as defined by the authorities of the institution (Fillingham, 1993).

People labelled as having mental health problems are not considered to be able to think for themselves, or even to consent to or refuse 'treatment', so once in an institution they frequently lose any attempt to resist it. Many people simply put their heads down, do their time, and hope the hospital runs out of beds.

Their freedom to move around the building, or to speak or make a noise, is restricted; their voices are not heard, as they are considered incapable of clear thinking. Control is exercised in the same way as it is in schools and in prisons.

The micro-historical constitution of one's environment, that is the tiny pieces of experience which go towards making up one's constitution or "self", is used by the institution to control behaviour. In 1837, Leon Faucher, a prison governor, focussed on controlling every intimate minute of an inmate's life. Before this, the mad were tortured and even killed if they would not conform. Foucault looks at this change as an example of the systematic use of power and authority in a society:

> *Leon's type of punishment does not indicate a lesser use of power... Careful control of every aspect of a life can represent a more complete exercise of power than a massive display of a death.*
>
> **Fillingham, 1993, p. 115**

Continuous and detailed control of children in schools is effective for the same reason. If children were simply beaten, it would be easier for them to recognise this treatment as wrong, and therefore to rebel against it. However, if you are under continual control and ridiculed for minor mishaps, the desired behaviour becomes embodied; it is much harder to recognise the oppression or the oppressor and therefore harder to resist. It is relevant that working-class children, who are usually exposed to more violent types of control and punishment, are the ones who rebel most frequently, whereas middle-class children, who have been continually controlled through all aspects of their lives, even though they may want to resist against oppression, find it more difficult. Minute and continued restriction causes much more confusion and makes one doubt oneself and one's thinking; this results in a clouded judgement about where the cause of oppression lies and therefore how to resist it.

Afterword

Laws and rules are not as effective in making people conform as subtle, continuous control of behaviour, as this eventually results in the desired behaviour being internalised as normal.

> *Power relations have an immediate hold upon the body; they invest it, mark it, train it, torture it, force it to carry out tasks, to perform ceremonies, to emit signs.*
> **Foucault, cited in Horrocks and Jevtic, 1999, p. 111**

> *The body becomes the mechanics of power. Soldiers are now trained to march. Factory workers now have posts, skills and timetables. School kids have to sit and write properly - insolence, lateness, laziness, dirtiness and impurity are punished.*
> **Horrocks and Jevtic, 1999, p. 117**

If you are in a mental hospital, you have your freedom of movement controlled. Doorways are significant; those who pass through them freely have higher status. The doors to the staff room are often shut; you are only allowed in if a staff member says so. Access to your own room is controlled by staff, as is access to the kitchen and food. You need to gain permission to move around the institution and are often not allowed to do so without an escort. Some people are simply not allowed out as their behaviour may offend a 'normal' person outside. The fence erected around a mental hospital is similar to the fences round schools and prisons.

Knowledge that may empower you is kept from you, for example your notes and information on your rights as a human being. You are then ridiculed for your lack of knowledge, as children often are.

> *... it is always the normal person who has power over the abnormal. The psychologist tells us about the madmen, never do we expect to hear the latter talk about the former - what they have to say has already been ruled irrelevant, because by definition they have no knowledge. [But that is code for not wanting them to have any power.]*
> **Fillingham, 1993, p. 18**

People in mental hospitals do not generally have any material possessions, except their clothes, a handbag and maybe a TV, as many of them have had to sell things to gain money, or have been institutionalised for so long that nothing belongs to them. They also have to give up their belongings if they go in and out of the hospital, handing over their cigarettes to be rationed or the money they have left to be monitored. This is similar to the system in schools.

They are also kept in poverty by the benefits system that pays them £13 per week. Most of them smoke to alleviate boredom and subdue feelings, and at £3 per packet per day, £13 does not keep them in cigarettes. This results in many people resorting to begging cigarettes and money from others, which is seen as "bad", "ill" behaviour. Work schemes have been set up, but the government's therapeutic earning rule prevents patients from earning more than £15 per week; this means that some schemes only pay £2 for a full working day. Schemes that try to pay more end up having to restrict the amount of time one can work.

Just as in school, popularity and resistance to authority are admired but feared; it is useful to be liked by the staff as you will be treated better and may gain more access to the outside world or to materials which represent power such as cigarettes, tea or food.

At Dockbridge, it is stated in the school summary of behavioural rules and sanctions that one must "stay calm at all times". In the mental health system, anybody who is not calm is heavily sedated, given ECT or put in an isolation ward; everybody is sedated to some degree everyday to keep them calm. In schools, Ritalin is being increasingly introduced to make children stay calm when threats and sanctions have failed to work.

If you are a patient in a mental institution, you have to listen to the staff, just as in school you have to listen to your teacher - they know best. Both children and people labelled as having mental health problems are required to explain themselves to a grown-up or a 'normal' person if they are thought to have acted inappropriately.

Sanctions

Sanctions for misbehaviour are similar in schools and mental institutions. In either type of insititution you can be grounded (if you had any freedom to leave in the first place). You have your belongings such as cigarettes, sweets and drinks confiscated or rationed. You are told off in patronising voices and you fear getting into trouble. You have a certain bedtimes and getting-up times determined by the institution in a hospital or a boarding school. The use of isolation wards is a similar punishment to the sending of children out of the classroom, standing them in the corner facing the wall or sending them off to work in another class.

Both children and mental patients bully their peers for not being 'normal'. Children are not popular when they do not conform to the standards of the majority, and people labelled as having mental health problems deride each other for not fitting into society.

Both groups suffer physical abuse. Physical punishment is used less now in state schools, but it is still used in many private schools and plays a large part in controlling children in the outside world and in families. It is still acceptable to use physical punishment to control people labelled as having mental health problems. A common form is electric shock treatment (Electro-Convulsive Therapy - ECT). There is no scientific evidence that ECT helps people to "get well" - it is simply physical punishment.

In the past, mental patients were tortured, but as the idea of illness has developed, and people have been seen as ill rather than misbehaving, drugs have been used more and more. This process has been spurred on by the multi-million pound corporations who are eager to put their money into 'researching' mental illness and establishing that it is treatable by their never-ending supply of new wonder-drugs.

In schools and in mental hospitals, people are monitored to see how well they conform to society's norms. They are subjected to reviews and reports, their behaviour is plotted on charts and they are continually tested. In both forms of institution, groups are refusing to conform to an irrational society and trying to hold on to their inherent creativity, zestfulness and individuality.

Normality and Adulthood versus 'Madness' and 'Childhood'

Young, old or 'mad' people are seen as (and often are, due to marginalisation) economically unproductive. As capitalist society is based on the production of profit, this means that they become a burden on society rather than of use to it. Only a normal, or adult person (probably between the ages of twenty and fifty) is seen as productive. Western society therefore values children and people labelled as having mental health problems only as potential people, potential profit-makers. It relies on the institutions to "fix" them so that they become valuable producers of commodity.

Children and people labelled "mentally ill" don't have to have done anything wrong. They don't have to have broken the law. They are punished simply because they do not fit into society's idea of normality. Children are seen as not yet having been made into persons, whereas "mad" people are seen as having managed to slip out of the of category "person". The mad inhabit a space that falls outside the adult realm, but they cannot be categorised as children because of their size and age; instead they are labelled "mad". Before the concept of childhood existed, children were simply experienced as people - small ones. As capitalism grew power relations and the forms of exploitation changed. Children came to be considered unprofitable so a special category had to be created for them. The definition of normality became narrower, and children and mad people, who had formerly been accepted as people in their own right, were redefined as outsiders who had to learn to become normal. They were no longer people, but only children or lunatics.

The Western notion of normality is also a direct cause of so many black people, asylum seekers, Asians and other foreigners ending up in the mental health system. They have come into this country from a different culture with a conflicting idea of normal behaviour. Only too easily are they categorised as 'mad'.

The Western idea of normality is based on the white middle classes. It is to be still, quiet, and polite and to be non-emotional (whether angry, excessively happy or excessively sad). The 'normal' person is well-educated and well-mannered (sufficiently conforming). Neither people labelled as being mentally ill nor children generally have these attributes.

> Pinel established a system of morality very much connected to the new dominant middle class as the absolute power within the asylum, and thus the standard for society as a whole. The danger of madness now came from lower-class people who did not wish to conform to this standard.
>
> **Fillingham, 1993, p. 54**

People labelled "mentally ill" have not quite embodied the actions considered appropriate for adults. Perhaps they have not controlled their movement or their noise levels sufficiently; in any case they have not sufficiently conformed. Many people labelled as having mental health problems are originally sectioned for displaying disruptive, 'unacceptable' public behaviour. They often have the same chaotic liveliness as children. Children move a lot, they jump around and make a lot of noise, they skip down the street. Because of our notions of 'normality' this looks very strange behaviour in an adult. Children approach and befriend strangers, they chat to them on the train and the underground, they rarely hide their feelings and openly express opinions on other people's appearance, moods and disabilities, for example. This open friendliness is often shown by people who are labelled as having mental health problems, but it is read very differently in an adult. In a child, it is innocence - "They don't know any better", "They haven't learnt yet". In an adult it is weird, mad, crazy, scary. This desire to approach, know and befriend fellow humans, who you

Afterword

do not yet know, without a "good" reason such as political, economic or romantic gain, is seen simply as "not quite right".

People labelled as mentally ill are often accused of "acting like children", for instance being emotional and loud, or expressing extravagant happiness, grief or anger. They are also frequently accused of having excessive imaginations, resulting in a diagnosis of having "delusions of grandeur" for believing they should have value in the world, or "illusions of persecution" for believing they should be treated well. People, including children, are not encouraged to use their imaginations, because their flexible, creative thinking could possibly lead to new ideas which might threaten capitalist society by exposing it as counter-productive for the majority of the people who sustain it.

Appendix One: Ethical Issues

Leah [helper] came to me and told me that the older children had told her that they had read my book and that it had nasty things written in it about her. [I had written down what the children themselves had said about her as she is seen as the 'worst' in the school]. Through the conversation I realised that she didn't know what I was doing. I tried to explain about my research and that I thought Ms Johnston [headteacher] had explained it to everybody in the staff meeting. Leah said that she didn't know and neither did the cook! I said that I would sort this out and also told her that I wouldn't write about her if she didn't want me to. She said she didn't mind if I wrote about her as she was "just doing her job" and "the cook should be told..." I said, "Leave it to me", and I'd write a letter to all of the staff explaining. I realise there is a dilemma here, in trying to get the children to trust me, and to prove I am not telling on them, I have let them read my notes and explained that the teachers will not, so they won't get into trouble. However I am also writing about the adults and letting the children see. I've decided that from now on I will keep my notes hidden from all participants.

Field notes, 1999

A similar difficulty arose when an argument started within the main gang of girls. They had been saying insulting things about each other and had they seen my notes it would have fuelled the argument considerably.

I had presumed that the information about myself had been conveyed to all staff through the staff meeting or otherwise, but this was not so. As a result of the incident described in my field notes above, I sent a letter to all of the staff in the school, and asked the teachers to make sure that all of the helpers in their classes got a copy. All admin staff, the premises manager and the cooks and dinner ladies received letters via the receptionists. I also made sure that people such as the PE and dance teachers, who only came in occasionally, were also informed. If I was in one of their workshops, I told them personally.

Children and Consent

Children have many gatekeepers positioned to protect them from the outsider who is seen to be a potential threat. This suggests that children are not responsible for themselves; the gatekeeper is the person who must be consulted. However, I view the child as a socially competent actor, so I wanted to gain consent from the children, the actual participants themselves. Is it informed consent if the child simply agrees because she trusts me as a friend, but is too young to understand what a research study is and what the implications are? With the juniors I found that it was best to explain what I was doing as I went along with each child, answering questions as they came up. If a child asked me not study her, or not to include some particular incident, I always agreed.

The way I seemed best able to explain my research to the infants was to say that I was writing a book about them. This gave them a clear picture of what I was doing, and also made them aware that others would read what I wrote.

Appendix Two: Summary of Rules and Sanctions

Classroom code of conduct

1. Listen to your teacher at all times, so you always know what to do.
2. Speak politely to all other children, adults and visitors.
3. Show interest in other children's opinions and their work, so that they will respect it too.
4. Co-operate with others. This means sharing equipment with other children and remembering to take turns.
5. Look after school property and furniture, like books, paintbrushes, chairs and tables.
6. Stay in your seat, or ask permission to move sensibly and quietly around the room.
7. Stay calm at all times and talk to your teacher (or a friend) about a problem.
8. Always try your hardest and do your best even when something seems difficult.

Playground code of conduct

1. Include other children in your games (especially if they have nobody else to play with).
2. If you have a problem with your friends talk and try to sort it out (instead of arguing or fighting).
3. If you can't sort something out or if you are upset or angry, politely ask an adult to help you.
4. If you do get into an argument or fight, always tell the truth afterwards. Own up to what you did wrong and say sorry.
5. Take care outside so other children don't get hurt. Apologise quickly if you hurt somebody by accident.
6. Look after playground furniture and especially plants and flowers.
7. Stand still when the first bell goes at the end of playtime. Walk sensibly to your line when you hear the second bell.
8. Rangers are older children who can help you play games and find friends - always listen to them.

Responsibilities of children

To illustrate through their behaviour that they understand the codes of conduct, and the importance of:
- Showing respect for others by listening and speaking politely
- Being honest at all times and willing to talk about problems and apologise for mistakes
- Showing kindness when others are upset or angry
- Moving sensibly around the school

Responsibilities of teachers

- To make sure that the codes of conduct are displayed in class and understood by the children
- To ensure that children have discussed, devised and displayed a list of class rules
- To foster good relationships with parents
- To contact parents to discuss difficulties children are having and praise achievement
- To recognise children's individual needs, social, emotional and educational needs
- To help children to develop a positive self-image and high self-esteem
- To make time available to talk through difficulties with individual children, groups or whole class - to help them see where and why things have gone wrong and how they might manage a similar situation better in the future

Responsibilities of all staff in school

- To be familiar with the code of conduct and point out to children when they are observing or breaking it
- To be consistent in their use of rules, rewards and sanctions
- To be fair and always willing to listen to both sides, explaining the child's mistakes
- To be a good role model for children
- To recognise when children are experiencing problems and work with other staff to help them

- To be positive and praise children's achievements and any improvements
- To encourage children to take responsibility for their behaviour and mistakes
- To investigate any allegations of bullying, before informing a senior member of staff
- To treat seriously any racist or sexist language
- To support other staff where appropriate in dealing with an incident

Rewards

For particularly good or noticeably improved behaviour:
- A child's name will be written on the class board or in a class book
- Parents will be informed verbally
- Their name will be written in the special Thursday assembly book, read out and they will receive a headteacher's award
- Any child receiving 3 gold stickers will take home a certificate from the headteacher

[Class teachers also set up their own reward system of ticks, stars, stickers, smiley faces or certificates.]

Sanctions used for misbehaviour in the playground

- Children will be told to stand next to the wall for a specified time for incidences such as provoking others, name calling, swearing or failure to follow an instruction
- For more serious offences such as repeated misbehaviour, stone throwing or hurting others, they will be brought into school to explain themselves to the headteacher or deputy. They may then miss a subsequent playtime, their parents will be informed if this is thought necessary
- Persistent disruptive behaviour will result in exclusion from the playground for a fixed period of time and parents will be informed

Sanctions used for misbehaviour in the classroom

Staff use eye contact and verbal reminders or warnings to stop misbehaviour straight away. If a child continues to break a rule they are told to:

- Move to work at a table alone
- Miss their playtime to finish work, or write a letter of apology to somebody they have upset
- Spend a lesson of half a day in another classroom or with the headteacher or deputy.

[There was also a system of pink sheets not mentioned in the policy where a child was given a pink sheet with the teacher's written remarks about their offence. The child took it to the headteacher or deputy. They had to write down what they thought they had done wrong and how they thought they should have acted. The teachers also wrote what they would like to happen, for example that the child to be reprimanded or sent to another class.]

When behaviour does not improve the following will happen

- Parents will be informed and asked to meet the teacher to discuss their child's behaviour and reinforce the school's disapproval at home
- A "behaviour chart" will be introduced. This details 1 (or 2) specific targets for the week and is used to monitor closely the child's performance in each session.
- All staff will be asked to help monitor the child's behaviour.
- The child will be made aware that a failure to improve will result in temporary exclusion from school

[There were many other forms of control and sanctions used that are discussed elsewhere in this book. The only one I shall mention here is that of physical intervention. When a child (usually an infant) refused to co-operate he would be picked up or dragged by the arm and put somewhere else. Even though this was not sanctioned by the school, it was frequently done.]

Types of behaviour which result in temporary exclusion from school

- Bullying, repeated physical aggression (such as punching, kicking, throwing of objects, scratching or biting), racism, stealing, vandalism or extorting money
- Persistent refusal to follow instructions
- Verbal or physical attacks on staff

A temporary exclusion lasts from 1 to 5 days, and is at the discretion of the headteacher. On the return from temporary exclusion a child and their parent must attend an interview with the headteacher before the child re-enters class.

In extreme circumstances the headteacher has the right to permanently exclude a child from school, with the agreement of the Governing Body.

References

Abu-Lughod, L. (1990), *"The Romance of Resistance: Tracing Transformations of Power through Bedouin Women"*, in *American Ethnologist*, Vol 17 (1), pp. 41-55.

Ball (1993), in *"The Ethnography of Schooling"*, Hammersley (eds.), Driffield; N.Humberside, Studies in Education Ltd, Nafferton Books.

Berger, P.L. & Berger, B. (1991), *"Becoming a Member of Society - Socialization"*, in **Waksler, F.C.** (ed.), *Studying the Social Worlds of Children*, London, Falmer Press, pp. 3-11.

Bourdieu, P. (1977), *Outline of a Theory of Practice*, Cambridge Studies in *Social Anthropology: 16 Series*, Cambridge, Cambridge University Press.

Durkheim (1964), *"The Division of Labour in society"*, New York Free Press.

Fillingham, L. (1993), *Foucault For Beginners*, London, Writers and Readers Publishers.

Foucault (1976), *"Disciplinary Power and Subjection"* in **Lukes, S.** (ed.), *Power* (1986), Oxford, Blackwell Publishers, pp. 229-242.

Gal, S. (1995), *"Language and the 'Arts of Resistance'"*, in *Cultural Anthropology*, 10 (3), pp. 407-424.

Geertz, C. (1973), *"Thick description: towards an interpretive theory of culture"*, in *The Interpretation of Culture*, London, Hutchinson, pp. 3-30.

Goode, D. (1986), *"Kids Culture and Innocents"*, in **Waksler** (1991), *Studying the Social Worlds of Children*, London, Falmer Press.

Horrocks, C. and Jevtic, Z. (1997), *Introducing Foucault*, Cambridge, Icon Books.

Howe, L. (1998), *"Scrounger, Worker, Beggarman, Cheat: The Dynamics of Unemployment and The Politics of Resistance in Belfast"*, in *Journal of Royal Anthropological Institute*, (N.S.) 4, pp. 531-550.

James, A. (1993), *Childhood Identities: Self and Social Relationships in the Experience of the Child*, Edinburgh, Edinburgh University Press.

James, Jenks and Prout (1998), *Theorizing Childhood*, London, Polity Press.

Kulik, D. (1996), *"Causing a Commotion: Public Scandal as Resistance among Brazilian Transgendered Prostitutes"*, in *Anthropology Today*, 12 (6), pp. 3-7.

Laerke, A., *"By Means of Remembering: Notes on Fieldwork with English Children"*, in *Anthropology Today*, Vol. 14, No. 1.

Mackay, R.W. (1991), *"Conceptions of Children and Models of Socialization"*, in **Waksler, F.C.** (ed.), *Studying the Social Worlds of Children*, London, Falmer Press, pp. 23-37.

Malinowski, B. (1932), *The Sexual Life of Savages in North-Western Melanesia: an ethnographic account of courtship, marriage and family life among the Triobriand Islanders*, 3rd edition, London, Routledge and Kegan Paul.

Merleau-Ponty, M. (1962), *The Phenomenology of Perception*, International Library of Philosophy and Scientific Method Series, London, Routledge and Kegan Paul.

Opie, P. & Opie, I. (1969), *The Lore and Language of Schoolchildren*, Clarendon Press.

Ortner, S. (1995), *"Resistance and the Problem of Ethnographic Refusal"*, in *Comparative Study of Society and History*, 37, pp. 173-93.

Piaget, J. (1971), *Structuralism*, London, Routledge and Kegan Paul.

Scott, James C. (1985), *Weapons of the Weak: Everyday Forms of Peasant Resistance*, Yale University Press.

Scott, James C. (1990), *Domination and the Arts of Resistance: Hidden Transcripts*, London, Yale University Press.

Silverman, D., Baker, C. and Keogh, J. (1998), *"The Case of the Silent Child: Advice-giving and Advice-reception in Parent-Teacher Interviews"*, in *Children and Social Competence: Arenas of Action*, London, Falmer Press.

Toren, C. (1990), *Making Sense of Hierarchy: Cognition as Social Process in Fiji*, London, The Athlone Press Ltd.

Toren, C. (1993), *Making History: The Significance of Childhood Cognition for a Comparative Anthropology of Mind*, Man. 28, pp. 461-478.

Toren, C. (1996), *"Socialization"*, in **Barnard, A. and Spencer, J.** (eds.), *Encyclopedia of Social and Cultural Anthropology*, London and New York, Routledge.

Waksler (1991), *Studying the Social Worlds of Children*, London, Falmer Press.

Willis (1997), *Learning to Labour: How Working Class Kids Get Working Class Jobs*, Hants Saxon House, Teakfield Ltd.